# Unleash Your Inner Creative Genius

## Master Creative Thinking, Spark imagination, and Transcend Your Limits

GIRENDRA NATH SINGH

# Your Free Gift

As a token of my thanks for taking time to read my book, I would like to offer you a free gift: Click Here or scan the below QR Code to Receive your Free Book:

https://gnsingh.ck.page/79606d929c

**Unleash Your Inner Creative Genius** is a captivating book that delves into the science behind creativity and provides readers with practical tips, exercises, and insights to unlock their own creative potential. Written by Girendra Nath Singh, a passionate reader, life student, and researcher of human psychology, this book aims to inspire individuals to make small daily changes that yield remarkable results.

★In this book, you will embark on an exciting journey, discovering how to think faster, smarter, and more creatively. Whether you are a student, employee, professional, or entrepreneur, you will learn how to design your environment, adopt creativity routines, and follow in the footsteps of the world's brightest minds to transform your thinking and predict the future.

Key highlights of the book include:

Understanding the workings of your brain, leveraging the logical left brain and imaginative right brain to achieve more with less effort.

Creating a creative thinking environment and establishing daily habits that supercharge your creativity.

Drawing inspiration from renowned creative thinkers such as Leonardo da Vinci, Ray Kroc, Maya Angelou, J.K. Rowling, Oprah Winfrey, Michael Phelps, Pablo Picasso, Thomas Edison, Steve Jobs, Elon Musk, and Albert Einstein, and exploring the creative techniques they used to generate innovative ideas and make insightful observations.

***Mastering 51 key ideas for personal creative transformations*** that activate your brain and generate a storm of ideas.

This handbook provides practical tools that can be implemented immediately, allowing you to tap into your innate creative potential. Say goodbye to burying your most brilliant ideas in your mind and take the first step towards building your idea treasure by clicking the BUY BUTTON above.

**Are you ready to boost your creativity?**

This eBook is dedicated to all creative minds seeking to explore their inner genius and make a positive impact on the world.

Date: 30th Sept'2023

**Girendra Nath Singh**
**Unleash Your Inner Creative Genius**

★ ★ ★ ★ ★

# Table of Contents


*Chapter 1: Introduction* ....................................................... 7

*Chapter 2: The Nature of Creativity* ............................ 15

*Chapter 3: Overcoming Creative Blocks* ..................... 27

*Chapter 4:  Cultivating a Creative Mindset* ............... 43

*Chapter 5: Secrets to Creative Genius* ......................... 57

*Chapter 6: Innovating in the Digital Age* ................... 62

*Chapter 7: Habits of Highly Creative People* ............. 68

*Chapter 8: Living a Creative Life Everyday* ............... 83

*Chapter 9: Top 51 Creative Inspirational Ideas* ... 103

*Chapter 10: Full Book Summary* ................................. 109

*Conclusion* ..................................................................... 127

*DISCLAIMER* .................................................................. 129

*ABOUT THE AUTHOR* .................................................... 130

*Thank You and a Small Request* ................................. 132

# Chapter 1: Introduction

**********

**"Creativity is the way I share my soul with the world."**
~ **Brene Brown**

**A Creative Thinking Story**

Centuries ago, a small businessman found himself in debt to a repugnant and old moneylender. The moneylender made a proposition to the businessman that if he could marry his charming daughter, Jennifer, then all of his debt would be forgiven. Jennifer was not interested in marrying the moneylender, but he had a plan to force her hand.

The moneylender took two black pebbles from the businessman's garden and put them in a bag. He then offered Jennifer a choice between a black or white pebble. If she picked the black pebble, she would be forced to marry the moneylender, but the debt would be forgiven. If she picked the white pebble, the debt would still be forgiven, but she would not have to marry the moneylender.

Jennifer noticed that the moneylender had taken two black pebbles and put them in the bag. She had three options:
1. To refuse to pick a pebble.

2. To expose the moneylender for cheating by taking out both pebbles, or

3. To sacrifice herself for her father's freedom by picking a black pebble.

Jennifer chose a pebble from the bag but dropped it deliberately into a pile of other pebbles before anyone could see what she had selected. She then said to the moneylender, "Oh, it slipped from my hand unknowingly. Anyway, you can tell which pebble I chose if you look in the bag for the one that is still there."

The moneylender was convinced that the black pebble in the bag was genuine and played along as if the pebble Jennifer dropped was white. Thus, he had to forgive the businessman's debt.

Although it is unclear if this story is true or fictional, the daughter's out-of-the-box thinking and creative solution to the rigged game is a valuable lesson in problem-solving.

The story teaches us that sometimes we have to think out of the box creatively and not always stick to the obvious solutions. Jennifer's quick thinking and cleverness saved her father from a forced marriage and freed him from his debt.

### Real-Life Examples

### Steve Jobs

Steve Jobs, the co-founder of Apple Inc. and a driving force behind the company's groundbreaking products, is widely recognized as one of the most prominent creative geniuses of our time.

Since a young age, Jobs has been captivated by technology and innovation. He dropped out of college in 1976 to co-found Apple with Steve Wozniak, and the two quickly gained a reputation for their inventiveness and innovative thinking.

Over the next few decades, Jobs' innovative ideas and products transformed the technology industry. He was renowned for his meticulous attention to detail, his relentless pursuit of perfection, and his willingness to take risks and push the boundaries of what was possible.

Among his many achievements, one of Jobs' most famous inventions was the iPod, a portable music player that revolutionized music listening. Recognizing the potential of digital music early on, Jobs worked tirelessly to create a device that would allow people to carry thousands of songs with them wherever they went.

Despite facing opposition from music industry professionals who believed that physical CDs and vinyl records would never be replaced by digital downloads, Jobs persisted in pursuing his idea. With the help of his team, he perfected the iPod's design over several months, experimenting with various shapes, sizes, and materials before settling on the ideal combination.

The iPod went on sale in 2001 and became an instant hit around the world, thanks to its sleek design, user-friendly interface, and ability to store thousands of songs. This product contributed significantly to Apple's rise to prominence in the technology sector.

But Jobs didn't stop there. With the introduction of the iPhone in 2007, which combined the capabilities of a phone, music player, and computer into a single device, he continued to push the boundaries of innovation. The iPhone changed the way people interacted with technology and paved the way for the rise of smartphones and mobile computing.

Throughout his career, Jobs was known for his unwavering commitment to excellence and his willingness to take risks and pursue his ideas even when others doubted him. He inspired others to change the world by believing in the power of creativity and innovation.

The story of Steve Jobs teaches us that passion and perseverance are essential for creativity and innovation. Having a brilliant idea is not enough; we must also be willing to put in the effort to make that idea a reality. We must be willing to try new things and learn from our mistakes because failure is an inevitable part of the creative process.

Ultimately, Jobs' legacy serves as a reminder of the power of creative thinking and what can be accomplished when our passions, talents, and determination to change the world come together.

**Elon Musk**

Throughout history, the world has been graced with many creative geniuses, from Leonardo da Vinci to Steve Jobs, who have revolutionized the way we think, work, and live.

Elon Musk is a name synonymous with originality, daring ideas, and innovation. He is a visionary who has transformed many industries with his unconventional ways of thinking. As one of the most successful entrepreneurs of our time, Musk's journey from a young boy in South Africa is a testament to the power of imagination and determination.

Musk's aptitude for innovation and development began at a young age. He spent countless hours teaching himself how to code and was an avid reader, devouring books on science, engineering, and physics. These early interests laid the foundation for Musk's future as a tech entrepreneur.

After completing his studies in physics and economics, Musk moved to the United States to pursue his dreams. He co-founded Zip2, an online business directory that offered city guides. Musk eventually sold the company for almost $300 million, which allowed him to establish other ventures like PayPal, SpaceX, Tesla, and Solar City. Musk's passion for innovation and his desire to make a difference in the world fueled each of these projects.

One of Musk's most ambitious ventures is SpaceX, which aims to reduce the cost of space exploration and ultimately establish a human settlement on Mars. Despite facing skepticism and criticism, Musk remains resolute in achieving this objective. In 2012, SpaceX became the first privately funded company to launch a spacecraft to the International Space Station.

Musk's other endeavors, like Tesla and Solar City, are also marked by innovation and creativity. Tesla is revolutionizing the automotive industry with its electric cars and sustainable energy solutions, while Solar City seeks to harness solar energy and reduce our reliance on fossil fuels.

What sets Musk apart as a creative genius is his willingness to challenge established norms and take risks. Many groundbreaking innovations have emerged from his unconventional ideas and approaches.

Musk's story is a powerful example of the transformative power of creativity and innovation. He has shown us that daring ideas and relentless pursuit of our passions can change industries and the world. Anyone who aspires to be a creative genius can draw inspiration from Musk's journey.

Elon Musk's story is an inspiring testament to the potential of dreaming big and pursuing our passions with courage and determination. His innovations not only transform industries but also hold promise for a better future. The lessons from his journey are invaluable and can motivate us to unlock our own creativity and achieve our full potential.

**What this book can do for you**

This book could easily be titled "Creative Thinking Stories" as there are countless real-life examples of innovation and creative thinking. However, I understand that you are not only interested in hearing stories, but you want to know how you can develop your own creative thinking skills to solve your problems and achieve your goals. You want to know how to improve your cognitive abilities to generate more creative ideas and gain an edge over others in providing solutions.

This book will change your perception of creativity and demystify the concept. If you can generate ideas that produce results, it has the potential to change the course of your life. You'll begin to see endless possibilities ahead of you and learn how to:

> **Understand the science behind creativity.**
> **Learn practical tips and exercises to unlock your creativity.**
> **Apply creativity to innovation.**
> **Develop a growth mindset.**
> **Improve problem-solving skills.**
> **Boost confidence and self-esteem**
> **Overcome creative blocks.**
> **Develop a creative mindset.**
> **Create new business opportunities.**
> **Develop creative habits.**
> **Enhance personal and professional growth.**

This list is just the beginning. I want to equip you with the most effective strategies to think outside the box and generate creative ideas on demand.

I understand this is a big promise, but the strategies in this book are not something I've invented. They have been used by many creative thinkers for ages and have proved to work. Creative thinking is for everyone, not just those in artistic fields or exceptionally talented entrepreneurs. Don't limit yourself to conventional thinking that only delivers mediocre results. Creative thinking is for anyone who wants to think and act differently to arrive at the best solutions more efficiently.

With that in mind, let's dive deeper into the concept of creative thinking in the next chapter before learning practical ways to think innovatively in later sections of the book.

# Chapter 2: The Nature of Creativity



**"The most important thing is to be creative and have fun."**
**~ Richard Branson**

There are countless inspirational stories of creative geniuses who have changed the world with their innovations and ideas, but one particularly inspiring story is that of **Leonardo da Vinci.**

Leonardo was born in 1452 in the town of Vinci, Italy. From a young age, he showed a deep curiosity and passion for art, science, and invention. Despite growing up in a time of great political upheaval and societal restrictions, he pursued his interests with unwavering determination.

At the age of 14, Leonardo became an apprentice in the studio of Andrea del Verrocchio, a prominent artist and inventor of the time. He quickly proved to be a gifted student, and by the age of 20, he had become a master artist and was given his own workshop.

Throughout his life, Leonardo's curiosity led him to explore a wide range of fields. He studied anatomy, botany, engineering, and optics, among other things, and used his findings to inform his art and inventions. He was known for his ability to see the connections between seemingly unrelated subjects and to use that knowledge to create innovative solutions.

One of Leonardo's most famous works is the Mona Lisa, a portrait of a woman with a mysterious smile that has captivated people for centuries. It may surprise you to learn that it took da Vinci 22 years to complete the Mona Lisa, and six of those years were spent just drawing her lips. This may seem like an excruciating amount of time to complete a single painting, but da Vinci's ability to connect science with art is what made him so successful.

Despite his many successes, Leonardo faced numerous challenges throughout his life. He often struggled to find funding for his projects and was criticized for his unconventional ideas. He also experienced personal setbacks, including the loss of his mother and several close friends.

Despite these challenges, Leonardo never gave up on his pursuit of knowledge and creativity. He continued to push boundaries and explore new ideas until his death in 1519.

Today, Leonardo is remembered as one of the greatest creative geniuses in history. His legacy serves as a reminder of the power of curiosity, perseverance, and a willingness to take risks in pursuit of one's passions.

**Understanding Creativity**

Creativity is the ability of an individual or a group to come up with ideas that are novel and useful. Novelty and usefulness are both crucial elements of creativity. Innovation, on the other hand, is the ability of a group or company to commercialize an idea.

Even though artistic expression is a part of creativity, it is not the only form. It tends to be applied to any space, from science and innovation to business and social issues. A certain amount of imagination, curiosity, and openness of mind is required because it frequently involves combining previously established ideas or concepts in novel and unexpected ways.

Through a variety of methods and practices, including lateral thinking, mind mapping, and brainstorming, creativity can be developed and nurtured. It is a useful skill that can bring about innovation and advancement in numerous fields.

Art, music, writing, design, engineering, and scientific research are all examples of creative expression. It is a crucial component of human intelligence that is frequently associated with characteristics like openness, curiosity, and a willingness to take risks. People who are creative are known for coming up with new ideas, thinking outside the box, and being able to adapt to new situations.

## CREATIVE PROCESS

**Vincent Walsh's** TEDx talk on **"Neuroscience and Creativity"** brought together a diverse group of creative individuals who shared their unique perspectives on art, science, music, and poetry. Despite their accomplishments, none of these creatives could explain where their great ideas came from. This is because creativity is a complex process that involves several components.

The creative process can vary from person to person and from task to task, but the majority of creative endeavors involve a few key steps. To study creativity, we must be reductionist and break it down into its component parts. These means are:

## Preparation

The first component is preparation, which involves years of deep thought and obsession to achieve one's goals.

This involves acquiring the knowledge, skills, and information required to generate innovative ideas. This should include education in a specific area or field, exposure to various perspectives, and trip with different problem-solving techniques. During the practice stage, people acquire information and know-how about the problem or task at hand.

## Incubation

The second is incubation, which occurs when the brain processes information in the background without conscious effort. The ideas and information gathered during the preparation stage are allowed to simmer in the subconscious mind during this step. Allowing the brain to make connections between seemingly unrelated pieces of information. It is a time for reflection, relaxation, and reflection.

This period of incubation is crucial for the consolidation of ideas, which occurs during the slow-wave phase of sleep. During this phase, the brain oscillates at about 0.1 Hertz, and events of the day get connected in new ways. Being prepared, being obsessed, and allowing for an incubation period are the three things one needs to put themselves in a position to have creative insights.

## Inspiration

The third is illumination, the "aha" moment when an innovative idea or solution strikes out of nowhere. It tends to be set off by different variables, like an unexpected understanding, another viewpoint, or a new methodology altogether.

This is a sudden flash of insight or instinct that gives a new viewpoint on the problem. Inspiration often arises from making new connections between reputedly unrelated thoughts or concepts. Insight is the stage when the "aha" second happens, and humans all of sudden come to be conscious of a novel and useful answer or idea. This can be a surprising flash of suggestion or gradual attention that emerges after a length of reflection.

## Evaluation

After an idea or a solution has been created, it needs to be looked at to see how valuable it might be and how feasible it might be. This entails looking at the concept from various perspectives, weighing its advantages and disadvantages, and determining whether or not it is compatible with the creative project's objectives.

In the laboratory, researchers use creative linguistic processes to study brain states before a problem is solved. By doing this, they have discovered that there are two ways to solve problems: logically or with insight. True creative moments usually come from insightful moments, and the origin of these moments is not always clear. Therefore, creativity is a mysterious process that scientists are still trying to understand.

## Implementation

This step includes transforming the thought or arrangement into an unmistakable structure, like a show-stopper, a piece of composing, a model, or a strategy. Implementing the concept and bringing it to fruition are required.

This is the implementation stage in the innovative process, where the concept is growing to become into a concrete form, such as a product, artwork, or solution.

## Reflection

This is the final step, and it involves thinking back on the creative process, figuring out what went well and what could be improved, and using the insights to guide other creative endeavors in the future. This step is very important for learning and becoming more creative.

## Is "Naturally Creative" a real thing?

There is a typical conviction that certain individuals are normally more innovative than others. Research suggests that creativity is a skill that can be learned and honed through practice, even though people's innate creativity may vary.

Studies have shown that innovativeness is affected by both nature and support. Although the environment and experiences to which one is exposed have a significant impact on the development and enhancement of creativity, some people may have a genetic predisposition to it. Creativity can also be cultivated through exposure to a wide range of concepts, experiences, and cultures.

In a nutshell, although some people may have a greater natural capacity for creativity, it is a skill that can be acquired, honed, and improved by anyone who is willing to work at it. It is important to note that underneath the bad hair of Brian, Bob Dylan, and Einstein, there was an average brain. None of these people were young superstars, and some of them were close to lifelong mediocrity. IQ has no relationship with creativity.

## Types of Creativity

There are several distinct kinds or categories of creativity, such as:

## Creative imagination

The capacity to produce original and expressive works of art, such as music, literature, or theater, is the subject of this.

## Creativity in science

In the context of science, engineering, and technology, this refers to the capacity to generate novel concepts, theories, or discoveries.

## Creativity as an entrepreneur

This alludes to the capacity to recognize and take advantage of new open doors for business or social advancement, frequently including the improvement of new items, administrations, or authoritative designs.

## Social innovation

This is about being able to come up with fresh ideas and solutions for social and cultural problems like poverty, inequality, or keeping the environment healthy.

## Individual creativity

This means being able to come up with new ideas or solutions for personal development, self-expression, or well-being, like starting new hobbies, doing things artistically, or practicing spirituality.

It is essential to keep in mind that these subcategories do not necessarily go hand in hand, and numerous creative endeavors may involve a combination of various forms of creativity. In addition, people can shift their focus or priorities over time and express their creativity in a variety of fields throughout their lives.

## Creative success can be influenced by several factors, including:

## Knowledge and ability

A strong foundation of technical skills and knowledge in one's field can help one come up with creative ideas and put them into action in an efficient manner.

## Resilience and Perseverance

Imagination frequently implies facing challenges, committing errors, and confronting mishaps. Creative success necessitates the ability to persevere and gain insight from these obstacles.

**Motivation and enthusiasm**

Imagination frequently requires a profound individual interest in the work, and having serious areas of strength in enthusiasm and inspiration can fuel the drive to produce and seek out inventive thoughts.
**Flexibility and Adaptability**

Creative insights can be sparked, and the ideation and implementation process facilitated by being open to new ideas and perspectives and able to adapt to changing circumstances.

**Supportive and collaborative setting**

In an environment where ideas can be constructively shared, critiqued, and refined, creativity frequently thrives in a supportive and collaborative setting.

**Experimentation and taking chances**

Imagination frequently implies facing challenges and exploring different avenues regarding new methodologies or thoughts, regardless of whether they are capricious or doubtful. Innovative creative ideas and solutions can result from taking these risks and exploring new ground.

**Uniqueness and originality**

Imaginative achievement frequently includes producing thoughts or arrangements that are unique and interesting, offering a new point of view or direction that separates them from existing thoughts or arrangements.

Overall, creative success is the result of a complicated interaction between personal factors like openness, motivation, and skills, and environmental factors like support and opportunities for creative endeavors.

### Business Case Studies

Creativity plays a crucial role in the success of any business venture. Surprisingly, there was a time when **Steve Jobs** was ousted from **Apple** by the board of directors, who believed they could lead the company more effectively. During this period, Apple experienced a decline in performance.

Under new leadership, the emphasis shifted away from creativity, focusing instead on analytical objectives. This approach involved reducing investments in research and development, setting aside promising technological advancements, and prioritizing cost-cutting and profit maximization. While initially successful, the company's inability to introduce significant product updates eventually led to its decline.

Apple found itself on the verge of bankruptcy, prompting the board to bring back Steve Jobs as a last-ditch effort. Regaining control of Apple, Jobs devised a creative solution that shocked everyone. Despite ongoing legal disputes, he approached Apple's major competitor, **Microsoft**, and successfully convinced Bill Gates to make a $150 million investment, effectively saving Apple from disaster.

This story highlights the pivotal role of creativity. It was a lack of creativity that pushed Apple to the brink, and it was a creative solution that rescued it. This lesson holds true for businesses today.

Without creativity, a business can only operate at half its potential. Creativity enables businesses to adapt in a rapidly changing economy, fosters innovation, and imparts a unique character to a brand.

Consider the entrepreneurial journey of **Ray Kroc**, the founder of the **McDonald's franchise**. Prior to venturing into the restaurant business, Kroc sold milkshake mixers. However, after encountering a mouthwatering burger at a fast-food joint during a delivery, he abandoned milkshake mixers and delved into the restaurant industry.

Likewise, the story of **3M** in 1971 demonstrates the importance of embracing good ideas when they emerge. The company's research team failed in their quest to develop a super-strong adhesive but, instead of clinging to their original plan, they accepted the failure and innovated. This led to the creation of the immensely successful franchise, the **post-It note**.

Business leaders must be open to embracing good ideas whenever they arise. **Kodak's** experience in 1975 serves as a cautionary tale. Despite inventing the world's first digital camera, the management failed to recognize its potential and even perceived it as a threat to their analog photography business. By not adapting their business model, Kodak eventually filed for bankruptcy.

The story of **Kodak** highlights the need for leadership that not only promotes creativity but also actively embraces it by taking risks and adapting to new ideas. A business that operates under the assumption that the world will remain static is bound to face challenges.

During times of crisis, creativity becomes even more crucial. It not only helps a business survive but also enables it to thrive. Looking ahead, incorporating creativity into the business model will be key to success for the next generation of companies. This involves investing in creative individuals, research, and innovative technology, fostering a work culture that encourages creativity, and consistently adapting the business to capitalize on good ideas.

It's time to dispel the misconception that creativity is limited to a select few. Everyone possesses creative potential, and it can be activated with some effort. Overcoming initial hesitations, one can embark on a creative journey by taking small steps. Engaging in morning pages, where thoughts are freely expressed upon waking up, can stimulate creativity. These pages don't require brilliance but serve as a form of meditation and self-expression.

The more you venture into self-discovery and explore the world, the stronger your connection with your inner artist becomes. It is crucial to acquire knowledge about yourself and your environment. Continuously strive to encounter new sounds, sights, smells, and tastes.

Whether it involves taking an alternative route home to discover a different part of town or pausing to appreciate the vibrant sky during dusk or the beautiful flowers along your work commute, seize every opportunity to explore something novel!

# Chapter 3: Overcoming Creative Blocks

**********

**"The greatest glory in living lies not in never falling, but in rising every time we fall."**

**~ Nelson Mandela**

A truly inspiring story of a creative genius is that of **Maya Angelou**, an American poet, memoirist, and civil rights activist.

Angelou was born in 1928 in St. Louis, Missouri, and experienced a tumultuous childhood marked by trauma and adversity. Despite the challenges she faced, she turned to literature and the arts as a means of expression and coping.

As a young adult, Angelou worked as a calypso dancer and singer, traveling throughout Europe and Africa. She later moved to New York City, where she became involved in the civil rights movement and worked as a writer and editor.

In 1969, Angelou published her first memoir, "I Know Why the Caged Bird Sings," which told the story of her childhood and teenage years. The book was a critical and commercial success, and it established Angelou as a major literary figure.

Throughout her career, Angelou continued to write poetry, essays, and memoirs that explored themes of identity, race, and resilience. She was known for her powerful and evocative use of language, and her work inspired countless readers and writers around the world.

In addition to her literary achievements, Angelou was a fierce advocate for social justice and equality. She worked with Martin Luther King Jr. and Malcolm X, and she was honored with numerous awards for her contributions to literature and activism.

Angelou passed away in 2014 at the age of 86, but her legacy lives on. She serves as a reminder of the power of creativity to heal and inspire, even in the face of adversity. Her words continue to resonate with readers today, and her life serves as a testament to the importance of cultivating a creative mindset to effect positive change in the world. And it reminds us that with hard work, determination, and a little bit of inspiration, we can all be creative geniuses, unlocking the secrets of our own unique vision and transforming the world around us.

Even the most creative people occasionally encounter creative blocks. Creativity is the engine that propels innovation and progress. These roadblocks can be annoying and demotivating, which can result in missed deadlines and decreased productivity. Fortunately, there are methods you can employ to get past these obstacles and resume being productive and creative. We will look at a few of the most successful methods for getting past creative blocks in this chapter.

**Know the Creative Block**

Understanding what a creative block is and why it occurs is the first step in overcoming it. You can't come up with fresh concepts or original solutions to a problem when you're experiencing a creative block. These roadblocks can be brought on by several things, such as stress, burnout, failure fear, and lack of inspiration. You can start creating plans to get past your block by figuring out what's causing it in the first place.

Everyone experiences creative blocks, but there is always a solution. Let's heed the wisdom of author **Elizabeth Grace** Saunders and liberate ourselves from perfectionism, allowing our creativity to flourish!

Feeling apprehensive about embarking on something new is natural, but rather than letting worries consume us, it's time to act. There are numerous methods to unlock our creativity, build up our courage, and venture into uncharted territories. If you find yourself stuck, experiment with different approaches in your personal life or business endeavors. By acting, we initiate transformation, and with each small step, we edge closer to manifesting our creative aspirations.

**Consider Taking a Break**

Sometimes the best way to overcome a creative block is to step away from the project entirely. When you return to the project after taking a break, you'll have a new outlook thanks to your mind's ability to be refreshed and your stress levels dropping. A break can help you refuel your creativity and get back on track, whether you go for a walk, listen to music, or read a book.

Creative insights can also come during holidays. I spent my vacations jotting down ideas for new experiments. I found that without the distractions of everyday life, my brain had the freedom to generate new ideas. Therefore, it is not a trivial suggestion to tell your bosses that you need a vacation for creativity. In fact, scientific research and business findings indicate that our brains need downtime to come up with new ideas.

It's worth considering that major companies such as **Apple, LinkedIn, and Intuit** recognize the value of allocating time for employees to explore new ideas and pursue side projects freely.

However, this doesn't imply that all your free time should be dedicated to creative endeavors disconnected from targets or deadlines. Taking breaks is also essential.

Allowing your mind to wander is a powerful method for unearthing creative ideas, as many brilliant minds have demonstrated. For instance, **Mozart'**s compositions often originated from melodies he conceived while taking leisurely walks, and **Albert Einstein** attributed daydreaming to his development of the theory of relativity.

While Einstein and Mozart achieved remarkable outcomes by embracing quiet moments for reflection and imagination, not all creative endeavors need to yield tangible results or ideas. Simply enjoying yourself more frequently can strengthen your creative muscles. Research indicates that incorporating fun in the workplace enhances creativity.

Researchers at the **University of Western Ontario** in Canada discovered that individuals exposed to uplifting videos and music clips demonstrated greater cognitive flexibility and problem-solving abilities. Additionally, a survey conducted in the UK revealed that employees who experienced enjoyment at work scored higher in creativity compared to those who did not.

By making time for fun and incorporating other aspects of creativity, you will reach a point where creativity becomes second nature rather than a deliberate process. Whether you are leading a business or striving for career advancement, you will undoubtedly reap the benefits.

**Change your surroundings!**

It can be beneficial to switch things up if you've been working in the same place for a while. Your brain can be stimulated, and new ideas can be produced by a change in environment. Alter your workspace to create a new environment or try working in a different room or location.

Understanding the challenge is fundamental to generating innovative solutions. If you've ever observed a curious child, you know how skilled they are at questioning everything. Follow their lead by asking numerous questions using prompts such as "what," "why," "where," "who," "when," and "how." It may sound peculiar, but executives at **Toyota** have employed this approach since the 1930s. By posing "why" at least five times, they uncover the root cause of any problem they confront.

Similar to thinking like a child, the final step in comprehending the challenge involves adopting alternative perspectives. You can gain fresh insights by imagining how diverse individuals, including colleagues, customers, billionaires, deceased philosophers, and even fairy godmothers, would tackle the problem. The more unconnected the person is, the more valuable their perspective. Expanding your viewpoint transforms your understanding of the challenge and unlocks the potential for brainstorming intriguing ideas.

Unleashing your creative side requires conquering the fear of making mistakes. When comparing children's creativity to that of adults, it's not necessarily because children possess a superior imagination. Rather, they are less burdened by self-doubt and fear to the same degree as adults. In this aspect, we can all benefit from adopting a more childlike approach.

Creativity is not spontaneous; it requires both structure and freedom. To maintain a steady flow of creativity, allocate time for it and establish a conducive environment. Like any other skill, you can't leave your creativity on a shelf and expect it to blossom. If you want to integrate it into your work, you must be deliberate about nurturing it.

## Get Inspired

Finding inspiration is one of the best ways to get over a creative block. Art, nature, music, and conversations with others are just a few examples of the many places where inspiration can come from. Spend some time learning new things, reading publications, watching movies, or going to events. Your creativity can be sparked and new solutions to problems can be produced when you are exposed to fresh viewpoints and ideas.

Both your intellect and emotions have a vital role to play when selecting the right ideas. In fact, when emotions are removed from the equation, decision-making becomes nearly impossible.

**Neuroscientist Antonio Damasio** discovered this phenomenon while studying individuals who were unable to experience feelings and emotions due to accidents or disorders. One might assume that these individuals would rely solely on logic, but it turned out that even the simplest decisions posed significant challenges for them. Without emotions, all options appeared equally valid, leaving them with no guiding force.

According to the **UK Institute of Practitioners** in Advertising database, emotionally driven advertisements are twice as effective as those based solely on logic. Consider it this way: Which is more likely to capture your attention—a life insurance ad that merely explains the affordability of coverage or one that vividly portrays the impact on your family if you were without insurance?

To bring your idea to life, you require confidence, a solid plan, and a constant supply of creativity. A research study conducted at the **Dominican University in California** asked 149 participants to either write down their goals or simply contemplate them. At the end of the study, 76 percent of those who documented their goals achieved them, compared to only 43 percent of those who merely kept mental notes.

It took **James Dyson** 15 years and over 5,000 prototypes before he finally perfected his groundbreaking dual cyclone bag less vacuum cleaner. **Walt Disney's** initial attempt to establish an animation company led to bankruptcy, not to mention enduring a disheartening 302 rejections before securing funding to establish **Disney World**. Without confidence, these creators would have given up at the first hurdle.

**Collaborating with Others to Fuel Your Creativity**
Getting over a creative block can be accomplished by working with others. Insights and perspectives that you

might not have had on your own can be gained by working in a team, which can lead to innovative solutions. The benefits of working with others include increased productivity and reduced stress.

Working with others can be a powerful way to ignite your creativity and generate innovative ideas. Highly creative individuals recognize the value of other people's opinions and perspectives, so they often collaborate with teams or groups. Collaborating with others can help reduce stress, promote a sense of community, and increase motivation and productivity. By working together, you can share ideas, gain insights, and achieve more significant creative breakthroughs than you would on your own.

A study conducted in 1990 at the **State University of New York** revealed that groups provided with brainstorming guidelines generated nearly three times as many valuable ideas compared to groups without guidelines.

In 2008, **Creative consultancy** Idea Champions conducted a survey to determine the circumstances under which people had their best ideas. The results indicated that both collaboration with others and individual work were catalysts for generating great ideas. Therefore, while teamwork is crucial, it is also beneficial to incorporate dedicated solo time into the brainstorming session.

Allowing individuals to brainstorm independently and then share their ideas with the group ensures that everyone's voice is heard, from the reserved intern to the outspoken executive.

The existence of **post-It notes** exemplifies this approach. When Spencer Silver, an employee of **3M (the parent company of Post-It)**, accidentally created a weak adhesive, he saw no immediate use for it. However, years later, product development engineer Arthur Fry realized its potential for temporarily attaching items without causing damage. Thus, the Post-It was born.

The more ideas you generate, the higher the likelihood of discovering a gem like post-It notes. By providing your minds with the freedom to explore, you will generate a greater number of ideas. This is where imagination and enjoyable ideation activities come into play.

**Practice Mindfulness for Improved Focus and Clarity**

It is the practice of being in the moment and conscious of your thoughts and feelings. Stress and anxiety, which are frequent causes of creative blocks, can be lessened by engaging in mindfulness practices. Take some time each day to practice mindfulness, whether through meditation, yoga, or simply taking deep breaths. You can approach the project with clarity and focus by practicing mindfulness, which can help you decompress and relieve stress.

Being present and aware of your thoughts and emotions in the present moment is the essence of mindfulness. Highly creative individuals often use mindfulness as a technique to calm their minds, reduce stress, and alleviate anxiety. By practicing mindfulness, you can improve your concentration, enhance your clarity, and heighten your awareness of your surroundings. Being mindful means paying attention to the present moment without judgment or distraction, which can help you stay focused, increase your creativity, and improve your overall well-being.

Any skill, including creativity, can only be learned through consistent practice. Similar to a muscle that requires regular exercise, creativity is a muscle. Make time to practice your creative skills by writing, drawing, or brainstorming.

You can develop a more attentive and observant mindset through mindfulness practice, which can help you see new possibilities and concepts. Permit your psyche to meander and create however many thoughts as could be allowed, without judgment or analysis. The ideas should then be evaluated and improved into something useful.

**Set modest objectives**:

Overwhelming goals or tasks can occasionally be the cause of blocks in creative thinking. It can be easier to stay motivated and less stressful to divide the project into smaller, more manageable goals. Track your progress as you go along by setting specific, attainable goals. Small victories should be celebrated because they can create momentum and boost motivation.

Remember, when you ask yourself, "How can you eat an elephant?" the answer is simple – cut it into small pieces and devour it one bite at a time.

**Try out some new methods**:

Your creativity can be sparked, and new ideas can be produced by trying out new methods. Try novel brainstorming methods like **mind mapping** or **word association** or play around with various mediums like drawing or painting. Your creativity can be sparked by the process of experimenting with new methods, which can help you break your routine.

Mornings are typically characterized by routine for most individuals. Upon awakening, we effortlessly follow a series of established actions to prepare ourselves for the upcoming day. This seamless process is made possible by our remarkable brains, which adeptly identify and store patterns in our thinking, retrieving them when needed. These cognitive patterns serve us well in our daily decisions and tasks, such as brushing our teeth or brewing a cup of coffee. However, when it comes to nurturing creativity, they are the least desirable companions.

Engaging in routine ways of thinking when faced with a novel problem only leads to unoriginal and uninspiring ideas. To break free from the constraints of unimaginative thinking and embrace creativity, we must liberate ourselves from reliance on these ingrained patterns and cultivate new strategies for our thought processes.

Consider this analogy: as the new year dawns and you set fresh goals, you also devise a plan to help you achieve them. This plan might involve adopting a healthier diet and exercise routine to shed pounds or embarking on a series of online courses and reading materials to acquire a new skill. Similarly, you require a strategy to alter your thinking patterns and unleash your creative potential.

You may believe that developing creativity is solely reserved for artists and musicians, but the truth is that it is a skill indispensable to success in any profession. In a world as predictable as our mornings, routine thinking, and unimaginative ideas might suffice. However, we inhabit a rapidly evolving world brimming with opportunities and challenges that demand extraordinary solutions. Within this context, creativity emerges as a near-superpower.

In fact, the 2016 **Future of Jobs report by the World Economic Forum** ranked creativity, critical thinking, and problem-solving as the three most crucial skills for thriving in the workplace.

Life offers us just one opportunity, so we mustn't allow fear to hinder our pursuit of a creative existence!

In our world filled with doubt and skepticism, deciding to embrace your creativity can be an intimidating choice. However, it doesn't have to be that way. Living a creative life is not about striving for fame or sacrificing your entire being to your craft. It's simply about living a life guided by curiosity instead of fear.

A creative pursuit is something that may appear unconventional to others, yet it ignites a sense of boldness, courage, or excitement within you. Whether it's painting, writing poetry, rock climbing, or cooking, it should be that special endeavor that sparks your curiosity.

Perhaps you already know what your creative pursuit could be, but you still feel hesitant. In such a case, it's your fears that are holding you back. Worries about lacking the necessary skills, thinking it's too late to start, fearing that nobody will appreciate your work, or feeling constrained by time and financial constraints—all these thoughts prevent you from doing what you truly desire.

So, how can you overcome this? We are often advised to let go of our fears, but, that's not always feasible. Instead, the best approach is to become comfortable with your fears. After all, they are only natural!

In a creative life, your passions and fears coexist. Your fears are welcome to join you on your journey, offering their insights, but they should not steer you off course or take control of the wheel. Fears are nothing more than passengers in the backseat, accompanying you and reminding you of the things you truly care about.
To break free from a creative block, it is imperative to confront these inner voices. You have every right to create, so give yourself permission! Declare it boldly: "I am a writer," or "I am an actor," or "I am a photographer." By doing so, you announce to yourself (and to the universe!) that you are wholeheartedly pursuing your passion, undeterred by any obstacles. Not even rejection can impede your progress.

Distinguishing between being original and being authentic is crucial. Academic titles and accolades do not necessarily pave the way for creativity, but life experiences do. The truth is you do not need a degree to pursue what you love. It is through real-life encounters that you gain the wisdom and knowledge to refine your craft. Take, for example, the author of the bestselling book **Eat, Pray, Love**, **Elizabeth Gilbert** whose personal journey of rediscovering joy after a tumultuous divorce became the wellspring of her literary success.

Her story is one of personal transformation, self-discovery, and finding love and fulfillment in unexpected places.

Elizabeth Gilbert had always been a passionate writer, but she faced her fair share of challenges in both her personal and professional life. She went through a difficult divorce that left her feeling lost and disconnected. Struggling with depression and a sense of emptiness, she knew that she needed to make a change.

In search of healing and a fresh perspective, Gilbert embarked on a remarkable journey of self-discovery. She decided to take a year-long sabbatical and travel to three different countries: Italy, India, and Indonesia. Each destination held a specific purpose that would ultimately shape her life and inspire her writing.

In Italy, Gilbert sought pleasure and indulgence. She immersed herself in the rich culture, savored the exquisite cuisine, and embraced the joy of living in the present moment. Through the simple act of nourishing her body and indulging in the pleasures of life, she rediscovered a sense of vitality and reconnected with her own desires.

Next, Gilbert traveled to India, where she delved deep into the realms of spirituality and self-reflection. In an ashram, she devoted herself to the practice of meditation and yoga, seeking inner peace and a higher understanding of herself and the world. Through the challenges and revelations, she experienced during this time, Gilbert discovered the power of self-acceptance and the importance of finding balance within.

Finally, in Indonesia, Gilbert found unexpected love and a sense of belonging. She encountered a charming Brazilian man named Felipe, with whom she formed a deep and meaningful connection. Together, they navigated the complexities of love, relationships, and the blending of different cultures. Through this transformative experience, Gilbert discovered that love can be found in the most unexpected places and that it has the power to heal and renew.

Elizabeth Gilbert chronicled her transformative journey in her memoir, "Eat, Pray, Love," which resonated with readers worldwide. Her story touched the hearts of many who were also seeking personal growth, self-discovery, and the courage to follow their own paths.

Through her honesty, vulnerability, and insightful storytelling, Gilbert inspired countless individuals to embark on their own journeys of self-exploration and embrace the possibilities of life. Her story reminds us that sometimes, we need to step outside of our comfort zones, take risks, and embrace the unknown to find true happiness and fulfillment.

It is safe to say that the invaluable lessons the author learned cannot be imparted within the confines of a classroom. Moreover, these experiences empowered her to pen her first bestseller. The lesson here is that creativity is nurtured in the vast expanse of the real world. All you need to do is embrace its endless possibilities.

Rather than striving to prove yourself as a "serious" artist, embrace playfulness. Like **Tom Waits**, who envisions his music as adornments for the minds of his listeners, you too can create art that is strange, comforting, amusing, intimate, or even angry. Some will adore it, while others may detest it. And that is perfectly alright!

It is never too late to embark on your creative journey. By embracing your fears, disregarding societal expectations, and finding comfort in your authentic self, you will liberate yourself to pursue the art you have always yearned to create. Approach life with curiosity, refrain from taking things too seriously, and you will discover that the process of making art has never been more effortless.

Creativity is not an exclusive talent reserved for a select few; it can be cultivated by anyone. By adopting different ways of thinking and navigating through the stages of understanding and implementation, you will develop the skills to approach challenges with creativity and effectiveness.

Embrace the joy in the creative process! Whenever you encounter a roadblock, indulge in something delightful. Engage in a game of basketball, take a bike ride, venture into rock climbing, or simply unwind at home with a captivating film. Remember, it's essential to find moments of relaxation to invigorate your creative flow.

# Chapter 4: Cultivating a Creative Mindset



**"Creativity is not a talent, it's a mindset."**

**~ Beth Comstock**

An inspirational story of a creative genius is that of **J.K. Rowling**, the British author who created the beloved Harry Potter series.

Rowling was born in 1965 in England and grew up with a love of reading and writing. After graduating from university, she moved to London and worked as a researcher and bilingual secretary. It was during this time that she began writing the first **Harry Potter** novel in her spare time.

Rowling faced numerous challenges in her early career, including rejection from multiple publishers and personal struggles such as poverty and depression. Despite these setbacks, she persisted in pursuing her passion for writing and eventually secured a publishing deal for the first Harry Potter book, which was released in 1997.

The Harry Potter series became a cultural phenomenon, beloved by readers of all ages around the world. Rowling's richly imagined world of magic and adventure captured the imaginations of millions and spawned a multi-billion-dollar franchise.

Rowling's life and work serve as a powerful example of the importance of perseverance, creativity, and imagination.

Despite facing numerous challenges and setbacks, she remained dedicated to her craft and continued to create stories that inspired and delighted millions.

In addition to her literary achievements, Rowling has used her platform and her wealth to support charitable causes, including children's literacy and research into multiple sclerosis, which her mother suffered from.

Rowling's life and work inspire us to cultivate a creative mindset, pursue our passions with dedication and determination, and use our talents and resources to make a positive impact on the world.

Innovation and progress are greatly aided by creativity, which is a talent that can be nurtured and improved over time. Those who are highly creative are not naturally talented; rather, they have developed habits and practices that help them come up with fresh concepts and solutions.

We will look at the routines and practices of highly creative people in this chapter, as well as how you can develop a creative mindset to improve your own creativity.

**Cultivate Your Curiosity**

Being highly creative often requires embracing curiosity. Creative individuals are always exploring new ideas, seeking different viewpoints, and pursuing unique experiences. Nurturing your curiosity involves being receptive to new opportunities, taking risks, and having a willingness to experiment. Embracing your sense of wonder can expand your knowledge, broaden your perspectives, and spark your imagination, leading to new sources of inspiration.

## Develop Your Divergent Thinking

Having the ability to generate multiple solutions for a problem or concept is called divergent thinking. It is a skill that highly creative individuals possess and is unafraid to explore unique or unconventional ideas. You can cultivate divergent thinking by practicing brainstorming techniques, such as mind mapping or free writing, to generate as many ideas as possible without analyzing or critiquing them. By exercising divergent thinking, you can train your mind to expand your problem-solving abilities, increase your creativity, and generate innovative ideas.

The greatest hindrance between you and your dream is your own mind. Many individuals believe that success is reserved for the privileged few and not attainable for ordinary individuals, causing them to not even try. This perspective exemplifies a point made by author **David Schwartz** in his book **"The Magic of Thinking Big."** The primary barrier preventing you from accomplishing your aspirations is not your financial situation or a lack of time; it is your mindset.

To counteract discouraging thoughts that deter you from pursuing your dreams, it is essential to engage in divergent thinking. To engage in divergent thinking, dismiss that logical voice in your mind. By doing so, you allow your mind to wander into the realms of creativity and innovation. In this state, you can explore the possibilities of what you can do rather than being confined by what you believe you should do. Once you have generated a range of possibilities, you can reintegrate your rational self to assess and evaluate your ideas.

**Establish a Schedule for Creativity**

Establishing a daily routine and rituals is a common practice among highly creative individuals, as it helps to stimulate their creativity. A creative schedule can help create an atmosphere conducive to generating new ideas, whether it involves activities such as morning walks, meditation, or listening to music. Developing a creative schedule involves identifying the activities or practices that work best for you and integrating them into your daily routine. By establishing a consistent routine, you can create a sense of structure that helps you stay focused, enhances your creativity, and maximizes your productivity.

**Embrace Failure as a Catalyst for Growth**

Failure is an integral part of the creative process, and highly creative individuals understand this. They perceive failure as an opportunity to learn, develop, and progress.

Embracing failure involves taking risks and not allowing the fear of failure to hinder you from pursuing your objectives. By accepting failure as part of the process, you can build your resilience and perseverance, become more comfortable with ambiguity and uncertainty, and grow from your experiences.

Risking one's safety and stepping outside one's comfort zone are often necessary for creativity. Even if you don't know what will happen, be open to trying new things and experimenting. Don't be afraid to try new things and take chances. Instead of viewing failure as a setback, embrace it as an opportunity to learn. Often, being creative necessitates trying out novel concepts and taking chances.

Try not to fear disappointment or committing errors, as they can give important learning potential open doors and assist you with refining your thoughts. Creativity can be stifled by apprehension of making mistakes. Instead, accept failure as a possibility and use it as a learning and development opportunity.

Instead of allowing fear to confine you to an unfulfilling life, overcome that fear instead of avoiding or disregarding it. It is natural to feel apprehensive about change. For many of us, taking a leap that has the potential to alter our lives can be quite daunting.

Undoubtedly, conquering that fear is necessary, and the initial step involves acknowledging it. Once you have acknowledged your fear, the subsequent step is to mentally prepare yourself, as this will enhance your chances of successfully overcoming it. For instance, asking yourself, "What is the worst that could happen?" can provide a valuable perspective when making significant decisions. Surprisingly, the worst-case scenario is often not as dreadful as anticipated, which can empower you.

Another effective approach to readiness is to "give yourself a carrot." By associating accomplishments with rewards, you can create a strong motivation. Promising yourself a reward for conquering your fear can make this challenging process more enticing. Breaking through the barrier of fear necessitates acknowledging its existence and preparing yourself to conquer it. Once you have emerged on the other side, you will experience a sense of reward, competence, and readiness to tackle any challenges you set for yourself. Even amidst success, it is essential to carefully examine our failures.

**Seek Novel Experiences to Fuel Your Creativity**

Highly creative individuals have a natural inclination to seek out new experiences, whether it involves traveling to new places, trying different cuisines, or learning new skills. Besides expanding your knowledge and perspectives, exploring novel experiences can provide you with fresh inspiration for your creative pursuits. You can foster a sense of curiosity and openness to the world by actively seeking out new experiences. By immersing yourself in new situations, you can challenge yourself, expand your horizons, and stimulate your creativity.

**To foster innovation, it is crucial to break away from conformity**

By embracing your inner Rocket Scientist, you can liberate yourself from restrictive routines. Rocket scientists employ first principles thinking, which involves systematically questioning every aspect of a situation until an undeniable truth is reached. For example, recognizing the need for raw materials to build a rocket. Throughout this process, it is important to let go of assumptions based on past practices. This mindset enables you to transcend established boundaries, such as the belief that only government-funded space agencies can afford rockets. As a result, you venture into the realm of innovative thinking.

To determine which processes should be challenged using first principles thinking, reflect on why you approach tasks in a certain way. When justifying your choices, ensure that your explanations are rooted in your present circumstances rather than past practices. Much like Elon

Musk, you may discover that by forging your own path, you can accomplish ambitious goals.

## Engage in Self-Reflection for Creative Growth

Self-reflection involves looking inward and evaluating your attitudes, emotions, and actions. Highly creative individuals use self-reflection as a tool to understand their creative process better and identify areas for growth. Self-reflection exercises can promote personal development, enhance self-awareness, and facilitate creative problem-solving. By regularly reflecting on your thoughts and actions, you can cultivate a deeper understanding of yourself and your creative potential.

## Create a Positive Environment to Foster Creativity

Surrounding yourself with people and things that inspire and uplift you can create a supportive environment for your creativity. Highly creative individuals have a network of friends, family, and colleagues who support and encourage them in their creative pursuits. Establishing a positive environment can help reduce stress, increase motivation, and promote a sense of well-being. By surrounding yourself with positivity, you can create a space that nurtures your creativity and encourages you to explore new ideas and perspectives.

Spend some time looking around and noticing the patterns and details in your surroundings. You may be able to cultivate a more nuanced and insightful perspective because of this, which may pique your creative ideas. Experiencing new things and going to new places can help you think creatively by giving you new ideas and points of view. Try to see things from different perspectives, accept new challenges, and try out new approaches and procedures.

**By shifting your perspective on uncertainty, you open yourself up to the possibilities of exploration**

A peculiar tradition exists among the engineers and scientists at **NASA's Jet Propulsion Laboratory**. During pivotal moments in each space mission, they consume peanuts. This practice originated when a Ranger spacecraft achieved a successful launch following a series of failures. On that day, an engineer had brought a bag of peanuts into mission control. Since then, peanuts have been consumed at every launch to ward off misfortune.

This tradition demonstrates that even the most scientifically minded individuals experience a fear of uncertainty. That's why we partake in peculiar rituals, such as eating peanuts or wearing lucky clothing, to regain a sense of control. This innate inclination is rooted in our evolutionary history, as fear of the unknown once protected our ancestors from potential dangers. However, when we completely avoid uncertainty, we limit ourselves from discovering new possibilities.

Scientists, on the other hand, do not view uncertainty as something to be feared. Unlike most people, when faced with a dark, shadow-filled room, they do not turn away. Instead, they explore the room until they find the light switch. Once illuminated, they can assess what they have discovered. The room may hold something intriguing, or it may lead to another door that opens another mystery.

To think like a rocket scientist means embracing uncertainty as an unexplored frontier that holds boundless opportunities for discovery. It is within this frontier that original thoughts and groundbreaking innovations emerge. However, this can only occur if you are willing to confront your blind spots and break free from processes and opinions that stifle your creativity. Once you reconnect with your innate curiosity and openness, you will progress rapidly toward your goals and lead an extraordinary life.

**Practice Your Creative mind!**

Allowing your mind to wander and daydream can help you come up with new ideas and perspectives. Give yourself some time to unwind and let your mind wander without being interrupted. Be open to new concepts and experiences and avoid making assumptions.

Asking the right question is essential to obtaining the optimal solution. In 1999, Ozan Varol received distressing news from **NASA** regarding the failure of the three-legged landing system he intended to use for a Mars rover mission. Varol immediately sprang into action, contemplating how to fix the existing system.

However, engineer Mark Adler approached the situation from a different perspective. He posed the question: How can we defy gravity to ensure the safe arrival of the rover on Mars? This led Adler to completely abandon the three-legged system and instead design a solution involving massive airbags that would inflate around the rover, allowing it to bounce multiple times before settling on the Martian surface. Ultimately, Adler's innovative design successfully delivered two rovers to Mars.

## The pursuit of productivity often hinders original thought

Genuine creativity requires time and space, which is why many modern work environments tend to stifle creativity. Many of us find ourselves trapped in a cycle of incessant work. Every email we send generates another email, which we feel compelled to respond to immediately. The pressure to achieve results and meet deadlines leaves little room for curiosity and exploration. In the process, we forget the innate sense of wonder and inquisitiveness we had as children, constantly questioning the world around us.

However, rekindling that childlike spirit of curiosity and openness is vital if we aspire to find innovative solutions to problems. Fortunately, reconnecting with our inner seven-year-old is not a difficult task; all it takes is engaging in a thought experiment.

This is why individuals like **J.K. Rowling** emphasize the value of boredom. In 1990, before smartphones existed, Rowling's train journey from Manchester to London was delayed by four hours. It was during this seemingly idle time at the train station that the story of Harry Potter took shape in her mind. Just imagine the potential gifts your mind could offer if you allowed it the freedom to wander.

## Take a walk with your question

The next time you find yourself struggling to solve a challenging problem, put on your sneakers and go for a walk. Walking puts you in an ideal mindset for innovation as it relaxes you and allows your subconscious mind to work its magic. Walking has been instrumental in significant breakthroughs for renowned scientists like

**Darwin, Tesla, and Heisenberg**. So, if you need to come up with an original solution, follow in their footsteps and embark on a substantial stroll.

**Create space for everything you truly desire by eliminating unnecessary elements from your daily life.**

Many individuals often lament the lack of time to pursue what truly matters to them in life. However, there is a good chance that we can accomplish anything we desire with a little life planning.

To begin, take a close look at your current obligations and determine which ones are genuinely necessary. Then, it's time to bid farewell to the unnecessary ones. As you redefine how you allocate your time, apply a filter to all the everyday responsibilities on your plate by asking yourself, "Why should I do this?" and "What will happen if I don't?"

Consider **Seth Godin**, who writes the most popular business blog globally. When asked how he manages to respond to every email he receives, he explains that he avoids watching TV or attending meetings, which frees up an additional four to five hours per day.

Best-selling writer **Haruki Murakami** serves as an excellent example of someone who embraced life to the fullest by organizing his life around his primary aspiration: improving his writing. In one of his books, he explains how this choice allowed him to focus on building a connection with his readership rather than specific individuals, such as family and friends.

While some may view prioritizing a few key areas as rude, Murakami's approach highlights the importance of being assertive in dropping many other commitments to devote most of your time to what brings you joy.

**Direct your focus towards creating work that leaves a lasting impact - work that will outlive you and contribute to a better world for others.**

While you have the freedom to pursue various paths in life, a life solely centered around oneself would likely be unsatisfying. Therefore, once you have deeply contemplated what you truly want to achieve in life, it becomes crucial to consider how you can enhance the lives of others through work that creates a legacy and makes a meaningful difference.

This is where the concept of legacy work comes into play. It provides you with purpose and fulfillment by engaging in actions that have a lasting positive effect on others. Irrespective of your past experiences or current life circumstances, you possess the ability to assist others in a unique way that would have been impossible without your influence. This is the essence of legacy work.

There are numerous avenues through which you can engage in legacy work. The key is to address the question: "How will this genuinely benefit people?"

Consider the example of **Dr. Gary Parker**, who resides in Africa and performs free reconstructive surgery for individuals who lack access to adequate medical care. It was when he first made the decision to help others in that region that his work began to provide him with a sense of meaning and fulfillment.

To stay focused on legacy work, there are several approaches you can take. For instance, you can establish a consistent benchmark for your most significant work, such as a goal of writing 1,000 words per day if your legacy work involves writing, or creating one set of sketches daily if you are an artist. Another method, inspired by **Jim Collins**, the author of renowned business strategy books, involves using a stopwatch with three separate timers. This helps ensure that he dedicates 50 percent of his time to research and writing, 30 percent to teaching, and 20 percent to "other" tasks.

Engaging in legacy work guarantees that what you contribute to the world will remain valuable for an extended period. Are you ready to embrace it?

**Take part in activities that bring you joy!**

 Engage in activities or hobbies that give you energy and help you unwind. Reading, listening to music, or practicing mindfulness can all help you be more creative.
You can learn new skills, interests, and points of view by trying out new experiences, hobbies, or activities. This may make it possible to think creatively and solve problems in new ways. Engaging in creative activities like painting, writing, music playing, or dancing is one way to grow your creativity. You may be able to discover new ways of thinking and unleash your imagination through these activities.

 Give yourself some time to unwind and refuel. You can unwind and reenergize yourself by exercising, meditating, or spending time in nature. Set challenging objectives for yourself and put in a lot of effort to reach them. This can assist you in improving your skills, overcoming challenges, and boosting your self-assurance, all of which are essential components of creativity.

 Keep in mind that developing creativity takes time and effort, but with practice, you can improve your capacity to generate novel concepts. Although it is possible to cultivate and develop creativity over time, creativity is not something that comes naturally to everyone. Keep practicing, be patient with yourself, and keep an open mind! You can increase your creativity and realize your full potential by incorporating these suggestions into your life. You can write down your thoughts as soon as they come to you in a notebook or digital document. You'll be able to keep track of your thoughts and ensure that they don't get lost.

# Chapter 5: Secrets to Creative Genius

**********

**"Genius is 1% talent and 99% hard work."**

**~ Albert Einstein**

**Oprah Winfrey** is a true inspiration when it comes to creativity and innovation. From humble beginnings, she has gone on to become one of the most successful and influential women in the world, and her impact on media and culture is undeniable.

One of the keys to Oprah's success has been her willingness to take risks and try new things. She started her career as a local news anchor but soon found that her true passion was in connecting with people and telling their stories. She took a risk by launching her own talk show, The Oprah Winfrey Show, which went on to become one of the most successful and influential talk shows in history.

But Oprah's creativity didn't stop with her talk show. She has since gone on to launch her own production company, Harpo Productions, which has produced a wide range of TV shows and movies. She has also launched her own cable network, OWN, which has become a platform for diverse voices and perspectives.

One of the things that set Oprah apart as a creative inspiration is her ability to connect with people and tell their stories. She has a gift for empathy and understanding and has used her platform to give voice to those who may not have had a voice otherwise. She has tackled difficult subjects such as race, gender, and sexual orientation, and has helped to change the conversation around these issues.

Another key to Oprah's success has been her commitment to personal growth and self-improvement. She has been open about her own struggles with weight, abuse, and other challenges, and has used these experiences to help others overcome their own obstacles. She has also been a vocal advocate for mindfulness and meditation and has inspired many people to prioritize their own mental and emotional health.

Oprah's life is a testament to the power of creativity and innovation. She showed us that taking risks and trying new things can lead to incredible success and that using our creativity to connect with others can have a profound impact on the world around us. She taught us to prioritize our own personal growth and well-being and to use our success to help lift others. And she left behind a legacy that will continue to inspire generations to come.

Since every creative genius possesses their own distinct set of qualities and characteristics, there is no standard response to this question. Because creativity can take many different forms and is frequently a highly personal and one-of-a-kind experience, there is no one-size-fits-all method for becoming a creative genius. While there are no specific "secrets" to becoming a creative genius, many highly creative people share certain characteristics and habits. Here are a few examples:

**Open-mindedness**

Creative geniuses typically have an open mind and are open to new experiences and ideas. They are open to receiving feedback from others and are not afraid to question their own beliefs and assumptions.

## Imagination

People who are creative geniuses frequently have vivid imaginations and can see things in new ways. They are capable of imagining possibilities that others might not be able to. They will generally have an unquenchable interest in their general surroundings. They adopt a lifelong learning approach by constantly asking questions, pondering novel concepts, and seeking out novel experiences.

## Persistence

Often, creativity necessitates a lot of trial and error. Perseverance and a willingness to put in the time and effort required to develop their ideas are hallmarks of creative geniuses. Despite the difficulties they face, they continue to work toward their objectives and concepts. They are willing to put in the time and effort necessary to achieve their objectives and are not discouraged by failure or setbacks.

## Willingness to experiment

Trying new things and taking risks are two common aspects of creativity. To achieve their goals, creative geniuses are usually willing to take risks and are at ease with uncertainty. Taking chances and stepping outside one's comfort zone is often necessary for creativity. Creative geniuses are not afraid to try new things or solve problems in a different way. They take chances and embrace uncertainty. They are used to ambiguity and see it as an opportunity for development and investigation.

## Passion

Creative geniuses typically take great pride in their work. They are dedicated to pursuing their creative vision and are motivated by a deep love of their craft. They are not motivated by external rewards or recognition; rather, they are motivated by a love of what they do. They often have a strong sense of purpose and a strong desire to create, and they are passionate about their work.

## A solid work ethic

Often, creativity necessitates hard work and perseverance. Creative geniuses are willing to put in the necessary time and effort to realize their concepts. Even though creative geniuses often appear to be naturally creative, they also put in a lot of effort to improve their skills. They can strike a balance between their creative impulses and the structure and discipline required to realize their ideas.

## Playfulness

A lot of creative geniuses approach their work with a playful and fun attitude. They don't hesitate to try new things, make mistakes, and have fun doing so. They approach their work with childlike wonder and playfulness. They enjoy experimenting and investigating without too much concern for the outcome. Whether it's in nature, art, music, or everyday life, creative geniuses are always looking for ideas.

## Spirit of collaboration

They frequently have the capacity to collaborate effectively with others and thrive in collaborative settings.

They are capable of recognizing connections between seemingly unrelated phenomena. They can combine concepts from various fields in novel and creative ways.

## Thinking across disciplines

 People who are creative geniuses frequently have a wide range of interests, abilities, and experiences that they can use in their work.

In conclusion, creativity is a multifaceted and complex phenomenon, and there is no one-size-fits-all formula for achieving creative genius. However, many highly creative individuals share certain characteristics and habits, including open-mindedness, imagination, persistence, willingness to experiment, passion, a solid work ethic, playfulness, a spirit of collaboration, and thinking across disciplines. Oprah Winfrey exemplifies these characteristics, as evidenced by her willingness to take risks, and try new things, her empathy and ability to connect with people, her commitment to personal growth and self-improvement, and her legacy of inspiring others. Ultimately, cultivating these qualities can help individuals tap into their creative potential and unleash their own unique forms of creative genius.

★ ★ ★ ★ ★

# Chapter 6: Innovating in the Digital Age

**********

**"The biggest risk is not taking any risk. In a world that is changing really quickly, the only strategy that is guaranteed to fail is not taking risks."**

**~ Mark Zuckerberg**

Innovation has always been an important factor in success, but in the digital age of today, it has taken on an entirely new significance. Innovation has altered the manner in which we live and work and has set out new open doors for imagination and advancement. We will look at the role that technology plays in the creative process and how to use it to drive success and accomplish creative objectives in this chapter.

**The Advanced Scene**:

The digital landscape is always changing, and new technologies are coming out quickly. Keeping up with the most recent trends and developments and recognizing the opportunities they present for creativity and innovation are essential for understanding this landscape. From social media platforms and online collaboration tools to digital design software and artificial intelligence (AI) applications, the digital landscape offers a wealth of creative tools and resources.

**Making use of social media**:

As a platform for idea sharing, networking, and audience building, social media has become an essential part of the creative process. Utilizing social media means utilizing the various platforms and their distinctive features to connect with creative community members, promote work, and solicit feedback. Creatives can explore novel concepts and trends as well as remain up to date on the most recent developments in their field with the help of social media, which can also be an effective research and inspiration tool.

## Online collaboration

Due to the proliferation of remote work and the availability of digital collaboration tools, online collaboration has gained popularity in recent years. Working with other people in real-time, regardless of where they are, and utilizing technology to share ideas, brainstorm, and collaborate on projects are all examples of online collaboration. Software for project management, online whiteboards, and video conferencing are all examples of online collaboration tools.

## Making Use of AI's Potential

As a game-changer in the creative process, artificial intelligence (AI) has opened new possibilities for automation, analysis, and innovation. Man-made intelligence applications can be utilized in different ways, from creating groundbreaking thoughts and bits of knowledge to mechanizing routine errands and smoothing out work processes. Additionally, AI can be used to analyze data and gain insight into audience behavior and preferences, allowing for creative decisions and success.

In the digital age, artificial intelligence (AI) has revolutionized the way we interact with technology. AI-powered applications have become integral parts of our lives, enhancing productivity, providing personalized experiences, and expanding our access to information. We will explore some of the remarkable AI-powered apps, including Chat GPT, Bard, Bing, and others, and delve into their functionalities, benefits, and the impact they have on our daily lives.

**Chat GPT**:

Chat GPT, developed by Open AI, is an AI-powered app that enables us to engage in interactive and dynamic conversations with a language model. By leveraging deep learning techniques, Chat GPT can understand and generate human-like responses, making it a valuable tool for various applications, including customer support, virtual assistants, and creative writing prompts.

**Bard**:

Bard, another remarkable AI-powered app, focuses on the domain of music composition. Using sophisticated algorithms and machine learning, Bard can analyze musical patterns, styles, and genres, allowing us to generate original compositions or receive AI-generated musical suggestions. This innovative app opens new possibilities for musicians, composers, and music enthusiasts alike.

**Bing**:

It's Microsoft's search engine, incorporates AI technologies to deliver intelligent search results and provide a personalized browsing experience. By leveraging natural language processing and machine learning algorithms, Bing can understand user queries, generate relevant results, and adapt its recommendations based on individual preferences. Bing's AI capabilities have transformed the way we access information, making it more efficient and tailored to our needs.

**AI-Powered Virtual Assistants**:

Virtual assistants **like Siri, Alexa, and Google Assistant** have become household names, demonstrating the power of AI in our daily lives. These intelligent voice-controlled apps leverage natural language processing and machine learning to understand commands, answer questions, perform tasks, and even control smart home devices. AI-powered virtual assistants have streamlined our interactions with technology, making tasks more convenient and hands-free.

While Chat GPT, Bard, Bing, and virtual assistants have gained prominence, AI is constantly evolving, and new applications are being developed. AI is being employed in areas such as healthcare diagnostics, autonomous vehicles, personalized recommendations in e-commerce, and more. These advancements continue to redefine the possibilities and capabilities of AI-powered apps, creating a future where AI is seamlessly integrated into our daily lives.

AI-powered apps like **Chat GPT, Bard, Bing, and virtual assistants** have demonstrated the transformative potential of artificial intelligence. These apps empower us with intelligent conversational experiences, enable us to create music effortlessly, enhance information retrieval, and make our lives more convenient. As AI continues to advance, we can anticipate further innovation and integration of AI in various domains, shaping a future where technology becomes more intuitive, personalized, and intelligent.

**Implementing Agile Techniques**:

Due to their emphasis on adaptability, teamwork, and rapid iteration, agile methodologies are gaining traction in the creative process. Projects are broken down into smaller, more manageable tasks using agile methodologies, and short sprints are used to accomplish goals and gather feedback. This strategy encourages creativity and innovation while also allowing for greater adaptability and flexibility.

**Trying Out Brand-New Technologies**

In the digital age, one important part of innovation is experimenting with new technologies. It implies being willing to attempt new apparatuses and stages and investigating better approaches for working and teaming up. Experimentation has the potential to provide new opportunities for creativity and innovation as well as new insights and concepts.

## Managing Digital Obstacles

While innovation has reformed the inventive strategy, it has additionally made new difficulties and dangers. Being aware of the risks and taking precautions to reduce them, such as safeguarding intellectual property and data privacy, and avoiding digital burnout, are essential for overcoming these obstacles. It also entails recognizing the significance of equilibrium and making the necessary preparations to disconnect and refuel.

In the digital age, innovation necessitates a willingness to embrace technology and investigate novel methods of collaboration and work. Individuals and teams can use technology to drive creative success and achieve their objectives by using social media, online collaboration, AI, agile methodologies, experimenting with new technologies, and navigating digital obstacles.

★ ★ ★ ★ ★

# Chapter 7: Habits of Highly Creative People

**************

**"Habits are the compound interest of self-improvement."**

**-James Clear**

**Michael Phelps** is widely considered one of the greatest swimmers in history, with an astounding 28 Olympic medals to his name. But his path to success was not always smooth sailing. Phelps faced numerous obstacles along the way, including attention deficit hyperactivity disorder (ADHD) and a fear of water that nearly derailed his swimming career before it even began.

But Phelps refused to let these challenges hold him back. He became a student of the sport, studying the techniques and strategies of other great swimmers and using that knowledge to innovate and improve his own technique. He also developed a unique training regimen that pushed his body to new levels of endurance and strength.

Perhaps one of the most inspiring moments in Phelps' career came during the 2008 Beijing Olympics, where he won an unprecedented eight gold medals in a single Games. But his success wasn't just about his physical abilities - it was also about his mental toughness and ability to overcome setbacks.

In the 200-meter butterfly, one of Phelps' signature events, he was nearly defeated by a lesser-known swimmer from Serbia. But Phelps refused to give up. With just inches to spare, he surged forward to win the race by a mere hundredth of a second. It was a testament to his mental toughness and refusal to let adversity get in his way.

Phelps' creativity and innovation have also extended beyond the pool. He has used his platform to raise awareness about mental health issues and to promote environmental causes. He has also developed his own line of swimwear and accessories, using his knowledge of the sport to create products that meet the specific needs of swimmers.

Through his determination, creativity, and willingness to push beyond his own limits, Michael Phelps has become a true inspiration to athletes and non-athletes alike. He has shown us that with hard work, innovation, and a refusal to give up, we can achieve greatness and overcome even the most daunting challenges.

The most held belief about creativity is that it's elusive, esoteric, and unique only to the anointed few.

The ancient Greeks believed that creativity was this divine attendant spirit that came to human beings from some distant and unknowable source, for distant and unknowable reasons. They called these spirits daemons. The Romans had a similar idea as well but called the spirit a genius.

Centuries later, not much has changed. The only difference is that we no longer attribute creativity to divine spirits, but to special individuals. We think that it's only Beethoven, Picasso, and Mozart who have creative genius.

Have you ever heard someone say, "I'm just not creative"? And, if you have ever felt that way, you may have a creative block going on.

There are many myths that float around when it comes to creativity; "oh, I'm just not at all right-brained" or "Some people are just born with it." Maybe they're born with it, maybe it's… their creative habits.

Is creativity something that some are inherently born with while others aren't? Is there any weight to the saying, "doesn't have a creative bone in his body?"

Let's look at what the scientists are saying:

**Left brain vs. Right brain**

You've probably heard previously the idea that people can be either left- or right-brained, with those who are right-brained attributed with higher levels of creativity. This is another reason why people often believe that left-handed humans are the most creative.

This was "conventional wisdom" for years; however, more recent scientific studies have overturned this idea, stating that it is far too simplistic. **Scientific American** reported that creativity does not involve a single region of the brain.

Instead, the entire creative process– from preparation to incubation to illumination to verification-- consists of many interacting cognitive processes (both conscious and unconscious) and emotions. Depending on the stage of the creative process, and what you're attempting to create, different brain regions are recruited to handle the task.

Neuroscientists who study creativity have found that creativity does not involve a single brain region or even a single side of the brain, as the "right brain" myth of creativity suggests; instead, it draws on the whole brain. This complex process consists of many interacting cognitive systems (both conscious and unconscious) and emotions, with different brain regions recruited to handle each task and to work together as a team to get the job done.

## Are some people born more creative than others?

Everyone is creative as a child, like **Pablo Picasso** once said: "Every child is an artist; the problem is how to remain an artist once we grow up." Children tend to explore, ask questions, maintain curiosity, and not be afraid to be wrong. We tend to put more inhibitions in place as we grow up, but this doesn't mean we can't develop habits to embrace creativity.

While there is no single set of " **Habits of Highly Creative People,"** however, there are certain traits and behaviors that are commonly associated with creative individuals. These habits can help foster a mindset that supports and encourages creative thinking and innovation: -

## Embrace curiosity!

Creative people tend to be naturally curious and are constantly seeking out new experiences, ideas, and perspectives. They often ask "why" and "what if" questions to spark their imagination and gain new insights. They actively seek out new information and perspectives to stimulate their minds and generate fresh ideas. Creative people are often keen observers of the world around them. They pay attention to details and notice things that others might overlook, which can spark new ideas and inspiration. They are interested in a wide range of subjects and are always looking for new ideas and inspiration. They are open to feedback and criticism and are constantly learning and evolving.

A childlike eagerness to learn and to understand is what all highly creative people have in common. For creative people knowledge is more than just information, it's a key that unlocks doors to new ideas. An insatiable hunger for knowledge (about your challenge or something completely different) will always provide you with novel insights and fresh ideas.

**Nurture your passion.**

 Creative people are passionate about what they do and often have a deep sense of purpose behind their work. They use their passion as fuel to fuel their creative process and stay motivated through challenges and setbacks. They prioritize activities and projects that align with their values and interests, which fuel their creativity and motivation.

Passion often stems from an experience or a relationship that moved us somehow and can lead to inspiration. It is often the emotional fuel that starts one down a creative path, but it's only a start. People who fulfill their creative dreams over the long haul balance the excitement about the future with realistic strategies for getting closer to their goals; inspiration with hard work; and dreaming with doing.

When someone advises you to "Follow your passion," use caution: aside from being one of the most common clichés out there, it's not very helpful advice. You must look for passion that is in harmony with your authentic self and is compatible with your other activities. Passion to prove yourself to others will probably not result in creativity, as it relies on your avoiding challenges that would otherwise lead to growth. So, while you should be open to what inspires you, don't follow passion blindly. Make sure it truly resonates with you and your skills.

## Embrace ambiguity!

 Creative people are comfortable with uncertainty and are willing to take risks and try new things, even if they don't know how it will turn out. They see ambiguity as an opportunity to explore and discover.

Creativity often requires taking risks and stepping outside of one's comfort zone. Highly creative individuals are often willing to take calculated risks and learn from failures. They view failure as a learning opportunity and are not discouraged by setbacks.

You can't think 'outside the box' if you keep placing things in boxes. Most people can't stand ambiguity and prefer clarity. This is a normal human reaction. 'Labeling and disqualifying' information is our brain's way to make sense of what we know. Highly creative people, however, have no difficulty in holding two opposing thoughts in mind. Working with a paradox will almost always lead to interesting ideas. It forces us to think beyond the obvious.

Creative individuals are not afraid to question assumptions and challenge the status quo. They are willing to take risks and try new approaches, even if they go against conventional wisdom.

**Practice Your craft.**

Creative people are committed to developing their skills and knowledge in their chosen field. They practice regularly and are always seeking to improve their craft.

Creative people prioritize their creative work and make time for it, even when other demands are pressing. They understand the importance of regular practice and the need to make space for creative thinking.

**Collaborate with others.**

Creative people often work with others to generate new ideas and perspectives. They are open to feedback and value the contributions of others, which can lead to new insights and solutions.

We're all familiar with how **Isaac Newton** discovered gravity. One day, whilst sitting under a tree, an apple fell on him, which sparked his realization of the phenomenon.

Yet, this tale is a great example of a common myth that creativity comes from out-of-the-blue divine inspiration. Although most of us accept this myth, it's wrong. Creativity doesn't just fall to us from thin air.

For example, Newton's discovery of gravity isn't exactly accurate. He, in fact, observed the apple fall whilst he was with someone else, which sparked a scientific discussion between them.

Their discussion involved reviewing what they already understood in terms of the phenomenon of gravity. Therefore, rather than Newton being the sole receiver of a sudden revelation; the idea surfaced from the interaction between two intelligent minds. It was only after years of intensive research that Newton could then finally put forward his mathematical formula on gravity.

Often, we view innovation as being the result of one mind focusing for a long time on one idea. Yet this strategy is rarely successful. Innovation often stems from many minds collaborating and influencing each other.

Therefore, to find the best chances to innovate, you should take an interest in what others are doing.

It's well known that **Bill Gates and Steve Jobs** didn't see eye to eye on the invention of the personal computer, but did you know that they both influenced each other with the PARC company and the Alto computer? Jobs saw the Alto on a tour of PARC, which encouraged him to create something similar at Apple and Gates found inspiration for the early Apple computer after working for Jobs for a short spell.

We can clearly benefit from interacting with another person, but even better for fostering creativity is working with large and diverse teams. As we now know, creativity is not the work of a lone genius, but of many minds.

In fact, when we look back at many famous geniuses, we see that they were guided by working with others.

**Thomas Edison**, for instance, worked with a diverse team from varied disciplines, such as physicists, engineers and machinists who dubbed themselves "the muckers." It was this team that joined forces and came up with some of

Edison's most well-known inventions, including the light bulb.

But why do we connect Edison with the lone inventor myth? Well, the muckers acknowledged the power of Edison's name, and thought it would be an advantage to them if they emphasized his brand and reputation rather than attempting to promote their own work.

Highly creative individuals often seek out opportunities to work with others who have diverse backgrounds and perspectives. They seek out others with complementary skills and perspectives and are willing to share their ideas and work with others. Against conventional belief, some of the most significant inventions, including that of the electric bulb, have come through collaborative efforts. Most such individuals bring to the fore different skill sets and temperaments, and hence the product is well-rounded. Creative people painstakingly develop their network.

**Stay flexible.**

Creative people are adaptable and flexible. They are open to new ideas and are willing to change course if something isn't working. They are not afraid to pivot or take a different approach if it leads to a more successful outcome. Creative people are united by their unwillingness to abide by conventional ways of thinking and doing things. In choosing to do things differently, they accept the possibility of uncertainty and failure—but it is precisely this risk that opens the possibility of true innovation.
The secret to creative greatness appears to be doing things differently even when that means failing. Especially during

the idea-generation phases, trial and error are essential for innovation.

**Engage in play**

Remember when you were a kid, and you could play made-up games for hours? Often the rules changed on the spot or what you were doing was more of a "stream of consciousness" rather than any kind of set pattern.

As adults, cultivating that sense of play is still important and can be a huge part of the creative process. One thing this allows you to do is to put any problems you have on the backburner, or "incubate" them as your mind focuses on something else. It is often in these times that the brain will quietly work away on your problem in the background, or the play will trigger a possible new solution.

Observing children in the imaginative play reveals a wellspring of natural-born creativity. When engaged in pretend play, children take on multiple perspectives and playfully manipulate emotions and ideas.

As adults, cultivating a childlike sense of play can revolutionize the way we work. Playful exploration can help stimulate creativity by allowing individuals to experiment with new ideas and approaches without the pressure of performance or outcomes. Learn to "play"

**Have a process.**

Creativity is a process. There's a system that one can apply methodically to generate good ideas. It's not an esoteric field that is the sole domain of the genius. But one must do the work, no matter how difficult.

A common myth is that creativity involves the "big flash of insight", whereas, as **Keith Sawyer** points out, there is a consistent process of deliberate creativity. Anyone can be creative if they follow a good process. All of the habits we talk about here could be contributors to a creative process.

**Take your hobby seriously.**

What is a hobby? A hobby is an activity you do and continue to do without any external incentive, whereas a job is an activity that has a clearly defined and almost mandatory external incentive. It often happens that as our careers take shape we relegate our hobbies to the more immediate tasks, such as growing up the corporate chain, and as a result, our hobbies are almost dead. Research suggests that there are several creative impacts of side projects.

Creative people know it all too well that hobbies are not distractions but are the very complementary mental and emotional deeds that help us in performing the core job better. Hobbies do not only allow getting things into perspective but also help us dissipate negativity and seek encouragement from things where we aren't getting judged harshly, unlike a job.

**Generate a lot of ideas.**

If you've defined a problem or problems and spent time learning or noticing, you're now in a much better position to generate ideas.

Creative people are often considered to have divergent thinking patterns, which allow them to generate lots of possibilities and even fuse different ideas to create combinations that are less expected. You can practice this kind of thing with mind-mapping exercises. The **University of Washington** also suggests you try keeping a journal, brainstorming, or free writing as exercises to encourage divergent thinking.

**Practice mindfulness**

Mindfulness practices, such as meditation or mindfulness-based therapy, can help individuals become more present and focused, which can enhance their ability to generate creative ideas.

While the capacity to observe the present moment without distraction or judgment is a vital skill for anyone who seeks joy and fulfillment in life, it's particularly important for creative thinkers.

A large body of research has associated mindfulness—both as a practice and as a personality trait—with many cognitive and psychological benefits like improved task concentration and sustained attention, empathy and compassion, introspection, self-regulation, enhanced memory, and improved learning, and positive affect and emotional wellbeing. Many of these are central to creativity.

However, for optimum cognitive flexibility and creativity, it's best to achieve a balance of mindfulness and mind wandering. Some forms of mindfulness may work against creativity—specifically, those that encourage one to let go of thinking rather than accepting thoughts in a more open manner. Interestingly, open-monitoring meditation, which emphasizes tuning into one's subjective experience, has been found to increase both the activation and the functional connectivity of the imagination network. So, try practicing an open-monitoring or non-directive form of meditation, and allow for constructive mind-wandering while also boosting attention.

## Solitude

The metaphorical "room of one's own" is a basic need for many creative people. Now, science has reinforced what the work habits of countless artists have demonstrated: Time for solitary reflection truly feeds the creative mind. Neuroscientists have discovered that solitary, inwardly focused reflection employs a different brain network than outwardly focused attention. When our mental focus is directed toward the outside world, the executive attention network is activated, while the imagination network is typically suppressed. This is why our best ideas don't tend to arise when our attention is fully engaged in the outside world.

It's important to make time for solitude, to give yourself space to reflect, make new connections, and find meaning. Unfortunately, solitude is widely undervalued in society, leading many people to shy away from alone time. We tend to view time spent alone as time wasted or as an indication of an antisocial or melancholy personality. But the ability to enjoy and make productive use of our own company can trigger creativity by helping us tap into our thoughts and our own inner worlds. So, don't avoid it...embrace it!

**Cultivate a creative environment.**

Highly creative people often surround themselves with an environment that nurtures their creativity. This might include having a designated workspace or creating a routine that allows for ample time and space to generate ideas.

**Experiment and iterate.**

Creativity involves a process of trial and error. Highly creative people are willing to experiment with different approaches and iterate on their ideas until they find a solution that works. Creative people understand that the creative process is iterative and that ideas often need to be refined and revised over time. They are willing to experiment and make mistakes and are open to feedback and constructive criticism.

"I make more mistakes than anyone else I know, and sooner or later, I patent most of them."—**Thomas Edison.** Edison was both a prolific inventor and innovator, producing over 1,093 patents. He was also a master at learning from failed experiments. When he died in 1931, he left behind 3,500 notebooks containing details of his ideas and thoughts. If you follow your curiosity, experiment with ideas, and learn from your mistakes, the quality of your creativity will vastly improve.

**Take time for reflection.**

 Highly creative people often take time for reflection and introspection. This might involve journaling, meditation, or simply taking a walk to clear their mind and generate new ideas.


**Seek out new experiences.**

 Creative people are often curious and open to new experiences. They seek out opportunities to learn and explore and are willing to step outside their comfort zones to do so.

Creative people tend to be continuous learners. They look for new experiences and new perspectives in their world. In fact, a drive to explore may be one of the most consistent personality traits in highly creative individuals.

# Chapter 8: Living a Creative Life Everyday



**"Living creatively means being yourself, not just complying with the wishes of other people."**

**~ Matt Groening**

In the heart of a bustling city, amidst the concrete jungle and the constant hum of life, there lived a remarkable individual named Amelia. She was an ordinary person with an extraordinary passion for creativity. Her imagination knew no bounds, and she possessed an innate ability to see beauty and inspiration in the simplest of things. Amelia firmly believed that creativity was not just a hobby; it was a way of life.

From a young age, Amelia had an insatiable curiosity. She would spend hours exploring the world around her, marveling at the colors, shapes, and patterns that danced before her eyes. She found solace in creating art, allowing her thoughts and emotions to flow onto canvas, giving life to her dreams.

However, as Amelia grew older, the pressures of society began to dim the flame of her creative spirit. She was told that creativity was frivolous and that she needed to focus on more practical pursuits. Doubts crept into her mind, and she started questioning the worth of her creative endeavors.

But deep down, Amelia knew that she couldn't suppress her true nature. She refused to let the world define her worth or stifle her creative genius. She made a vow to herself, a pact to live a creative life every day, no matter what.

With unwavering determination, Amelia embarked on a journey of self-discovery and creative awakening. She sought out like-minded individuals who shared her passion and vision. She joined art communities, attended workshops, and immersed herself in the creative energy that surrounded her. These connections fueled her creativity, pushing her beyond her limits and inspiring her to explore new mediums and techniques.

Amelia understood that creativity was not just about the act of creating. It was a mindset, a way of approaching life with an open heart and an open mind. She started seeing inspiration in the mundane, finding beauty in the ordinary, and weaving stories from the threads of her daily experiences.

She discovered that living a creative life every day meant embracing failure as a stepping stone to success. Amelia learned to celebrate her mistakes, knowing that they were valuable lessons in disguise. She realized that the journey of a creative person was not always smooth, but it was the bumps and detours that made it even more rewarding.

As Amelia continued her creative path, she found herself not only creating for herself but also for others. She realized the profound impact that her work could have on the world, how it could touch hearts, provoke thoughts, and inspire change. Her art became a vessel for her voice, a medium to express her values, dreams, and aspirations.

Amelia's commitment to living a creative life every day became contagious. She encouraged those around her to embrace their own creative spark, igniting a flame of inspiration that spread far and wide. Through her example, she showed others that creativity was not limited to artists alone; it was accessible to everyone, in every facet of life.

Amelia's story is a testament to the power of living a creative life every day. It reminds us that within each of us lies a wellspring of imagination, waiting to be unleashed. It teaches us to find joy in the process, to embrace the unknown, and to cultivate a mindset that nurtures creativity.

So, dear reader, as you embark on your own creative journey, remember Amelia's story. Let it inspire you to **Unleash Your Creative Genius** and live a life that celebrates the boundless possibilities of imagination. For in embracing your creativity, you'll discover the true essence of what it means to be alive.

Innovation is fueled by creativity. Without it, new concepts would never emerge, and development would stagnate. However, creativity alone is insufficient. We must also learn how to put our ideas into action and bring them to life in the real world if we want to have an impact that lasts. How to bring creativity to life, put ideas into action, and have an impact that lasts will be the focus of this chapter.

**Setting Your Objectives and Vision**

You need to have well-defined objectives and a clear vision of what you want to accomplish before you can put your ideas into action. This implies asking yourself what you need to achieve, what achievement resembles, and what explicit results you desire to accomplish.

**Choosing Your Sources**

You need to determine the resources you will require to bring your ideas to life. This incorporates all that from time and cash to ability, innovation, and backing from others.

**Fostering an Arrangement**

When you have an unmistakable vision and assets, you want to foster an arrangement for rejuvenating your thoughts. This means creating a timetable for achieving your goals and breaking them down into smaller, more manageable steps. It likewise implies recognizing possible snags and creating alternate courses of action for defeating them.

**Developing a Creative Attitude**

You need to cultivate a creative mindset to see the world in new and creative ways in order to realize your ideas. This requires accepting ambiguity and unpredictability, being open to novel strategies and concepts, and remaining engaged and curious.

**Organizing a Team**

Often, others need to help you and work with you to bring your ideas to life. To build a team, you need to find people who have the knowledge and skills you need to bring your ideas to life and hire them to help you succeed.

## Communicating with Ease

If you want your ideas to come to life, communication is essential. This requires you to articulate your vision and objectives in detail, share your progress and milestones, and solicit other people's feedback and input. It also entails actively listening to feedback and criticism and thoughtfully responding to it.

## Making a move

At last, rejuvenating your thoughts requires making a move. This entails carrying out your strategy, progressing toward your objectives, and continuously improving your approach. It also entails accepting failure as a learning opportunity and taking risks.

## Assessing Performance and Making Adjustments

You need to keep track of your progress and make any necessary adjustments to have an impact that lasts. This entails establishing targets for success, keeping track of your progress, and adapting your strategy in response to what is successful and what is not.

## Embrace the Flow of Creative Inspiration

To tap into the wellspring of creative inspiration, all it takes is opening yourself up to the possibilities. Begin by becoming attuned to the world unfolding around you. The next time you commute or take a leisurely stroll through your neighborhood, set aside your phone, and remove your headphones. Let the breeze caress your cheek and tune in to the snippets of conversation floating around you. Observe the eclectic attire your neighbor dons while mowing the lawn and admire the stark beauty of even the wintriest forest scene.

As an artist, it is your calling to foster a receptive and open mindset toward the world. Sharpen your senses and heighten your awareness, allowing yourself to be receptive to the universe's gentle nudges, unexpected surprises, and subtle hints that constantly surround you. Acknowledge that the creation of art is not a solitary endeavor but a collaborative dance between you and the world.

Cultivating a practice of awareness involves finding regular moments throughout your day to pause and reflect. Dedicate a few extra minutes each morning to remain in bed, taking deep breaths and connecting with the sensations of your body. Transform your daily commute by choosing to walk to your workplace, rather than opting for a cab. And before you retire for the night, indulge in the experience of listening to music with closed eyes. By seamlessly integrating the habit of awareness into your existing routine, you can gradually make it an intrinsic part of your life. With time and practice, you will notice this heightened state of awareness becoming second nature to you.

In this state of receptivity, you will witness the world in its vibrant glory, discovering inspiration in the seemingly ordinary moments that surround you. Embrace the flow of creative energy that emanates from the universe, and let it guide your artistic journey. By nourishing your connection to the world and embracing the beauty of each passing moment, you will unlock the boundless depths of your creative genius.

# Nurturing a Connection with the Nature

It is essential to cultivate a profound bond with the creative impulse that resides within us. Inspiration can arise from a myriad of sources, ranging from the depths of suffering to the wonders of nature or the embrace of love. But what exactly is this enigmatic force that propels us to reach for a pen, a paintbrush, or a camera? Where does its origins lie?

Deborah refers to it as the creative impulse, recognizing its significance in our artistic endeavors. She firmly believes that fostering a relationship with this innate drive is pivotal to our creative practice.

The arrival of the creative impulse cannot always be predicted or controlled. However, one thing is certain: if we choose to ignore it when it emerges, it gradually retreats, making fewer appearances over time. Conversely, if we heed its call, our connection with it will flourish, much like any relationship. Therefore, it becomes imperative to discover ways to open ourselves up to its influence and to wholeheartedly embrace its presence. By doing so, we not only honor our deep well of creativity but also allow it to thrive.

Acknowledge that the creative impulse is an ever-present force, seeking an outlet for expression. Embrace its visits, whether they arrive as a gentle whisper or an intense surge of inspiration. When you engage with this force, you embark on a journey of discovery and growth, fueling the flame of creativity within you.

Celebrate your unique ability to tap into this wellspring of creativity, for it holds the power to illuminate your artistic path. Nurture the relationship with the creative impulse, and watch as it blossoms, infusing your artistic practice with depth, richness, and fulfillment.

## Embrace Daily Creativity: Unleashing Your Unique Perspective

To tap into your creativity daily, it is crucial to dedicate time to pause and observe the world around you. The first step towards cultivating a more creative mindset lies in fostering a passion for curiosity. As we grow older, the routine of life often dulls our sense of wonder. However, creative individuals continue to nurture their curiosity, even well into their golden years.

Stay curious! Make a conscious effort to seek out something that surprises you each day. Take a moment to pause, allowing yourself to savor new experiences, such as trying a different dish from the restaurant menu or genuinely listening to your colleagues at the office. Remember, every moment holds the potential for discovery and learning, no matter how seemingly insignificant. Keep your mind open to the possibilities that surround you.

Once you awaken your creativity, it becomes vital to shield it from distractions. Creative individuals develop habits that enable them to focus their attention and eliminate anything that hinders their progress.

Take control of your personal schedule, ensuring that your daily activities align with your creative goals. Consider when you are most productive—whether it's during the early morning hours or late at night—and allocate dedicated time to focus when your energy is at its peak.

Protect this time and use it to immerse yourself in creative endeavors.

Above all, nurture and foster your unique way of thinking. Embrace your individual perspective and allow it to shape your creative process. By cultivating a mindset that supports and values your distinct approach to the world, creativity will seamlessly intertwine with every aspect of your life.

Embrace the wonders of curiosity, protect your creative sanctuary from distractions, and nurture your unique thinking. As you make these intentional choices, creativity will flourish, transforming into an integral part of your daily existence.

## Create an Inspiring Work Environment: Balancing Space and Exploration

To unleash your creativity to its fullest potential, it is essential to curate an inspiring work environment tailored to your needs. However, remember not to confine yourself solely to that space—occasionally venture beyond its boundaries as well.

Begin by thoughtfully designing your home environment, ensuring that it fosters creativity in every corner. Additionally, pay special attention to your workspace, as it should cater to all aspects of your creative process. Personalize this space to reflect your unique style and preferences.

Craft a workspace that accommodates your specific creative requirements. Reflect on the kind of environment in which you thrive and experiment with different setups to find the ideal one for you. Invest the effort into building a space that inspires and nurtures your creative flow.

In addition to creating a conducive physical environment, tap into your inner child to invigorate your creative process. Embracing your inner child can act as a catalyst for your projects, infusing them with energy and enthusiasm.

Foster a Kid-Thinking mindset, which places emphasis on play and curiosity. This approach unlocks the powerful creative potential within us, helping us overcome obstacles and limitations. Engaging in playful activities stimulates our minds and encourages new connections and ideas to flourish. Moreover, Kid-Thinking keeps us grounded in the present moment, fostering a positive mindset in our search for creativity and innovative solutions.

By practicing composure and staying present, you can make conscious and confident decisions. Direct your energy towards positivity and channel it into further creative endeavors. Embracing your inner child and adopting a Kid-Thinking mindset will infuse your creative journey with joy, spontaneity, and a fresh perspective.

Remember, while creating an inspiring workspace is vital, it's equally important to venture beyond its confines. Explore the world around you, seeking inspiration from diverse sources. Engage with new experiences, people, and environments, allowing them to fuel your creative fire. By striking a balance between your dedicated workspace and the wider world, you will unlock a wealth of creative possibilities and elevate your artistic expression to new heights.

**Regularly disconnect from technology**

Make it a habit to regularly detach yourself from modern technology. Challenge yourself to abstain from using it for at least four hours every day. By undertaking this technology detox, you will create space to reconnect with your thoughts and those closest to you. Prepare to be astonished by the heightened focus you will experience. With this newfound clarity, you can dedicate your attention to manifesting the life you envision. Not only that, but you may also notice a surge in your energy levels, invigorating your pursuit of creativity and personal growth.

**Nurture Your Hobbies and Side Projects Alongside Your Artistic Journey**

When you embark on your artistic path, it's vital not to neglect your hobbies and side projects. These endeavors serve as valuable outlets when you encounter creative blocks along the way.

Creativity and inspiration often arise when we allow our minds to wander freely. Therefore, it is beneficial to have backup projects that can divert your attention from your central pursuit. Engaging in these supplementary endeavors creates the necessary mental space for innovative thinking to thrive.

Maintaining your hobbies is not only about combating creative blocks; it holds deeper significance. Abandoning your hobbies can leave you feeling unfulfilled. How can you truly unlock your creative potential if you deny yourself the opportunity to take breaks and enjoy other activities? No matter how devoted you are to your primary artistic project, denying yourself leisure and recreation will inevitably leave a void in your life.

By nurturing your hobbies and side projects alongside your artistic endeavors, you create a harmonious balance. These activities provide not only respite and enjoyment but also allow you to recharge and gain fresh perspectives. They enrich your creative journey by infusing it with diverse experiences and insights, ultimately enhancing the quality of your artistry.

**Embrace the Benefits of Obscurity Before Sharing Your Work**

The state of obscurity grants you a valuable opportunity for creative exploration and the freedom to make mistakes. When your work remains unknown, you have the space to take risks and refine your craft without the weight of external scrutiny. It is during this period that you can truly embrace experimentation, unencumbered by the expectations and pressures that come with recognition.

Sharing your work with others and becoming well-known brings forth a different set of challenges. As your audience grows, every aspect of your art will be scrutinized, and the pressure to consistently produce "great" work intensifies. The weight of expectations can hinder your willingness to explore new territories, fearing potential backlash or disappointment from your audience. Even if you attempt something innovative that doesn't quite resonate, there may be critics voicing their disapproval.

However, when you exist in relative obscurity, you are liberated from these constraints. With no one knowing about you, you have the freedom to pursue any creative path you desire and learn from the inevitable mistakes that arise along the way. This period allows for uninhibited growth and self-discovery.

As your artistic journey progresses, it becomes crucial to share your work with others. Establishing a blog, website, or utilizing online platforms to showcase your creations becomes an essential step in your artistic development. Sharing your work allows you to connect with like-minded individuals, receive valuable feedback, and expand your reach. However, it is important to recognize and cherish the benefits of obscurity that have nurtured your creative exploration thus far.

Strive to find a balance between the solitude of obscurity and the exposure of sharing your work. Embrace the obscurity phase to experiment fearlessly, learn from your mistakes, and refine your artistic voice. Then, when the time feels right, step into the realm of sharing, allowing your unique perspective to be appreciated and recognized by a wider audience.

## Align Your Daily Routine with Your Body's Natural Rhythms

Creating a daily routine that harmonizes with your body's natural rhythms is key to optimizing your productivity and creativity. Often, we unconsciously start our day by checking emails, assuming it's a productive move. However, this can hinder overall efficiency.

Our bodies follow a circadian rhythm, a 24-hour cycle where our energy levels fluctuate. Mornings tend to be the time when we are most alert and effective. Therefore, it is advisable to reserve this precious time for important or challenging tasks that require focused attention.

Engaging in email responses or attending to phone calls during this prime period means allocating your peak productivity time to other people's priorities. Consequently, when you finally turn your attention to your own projects, you may find yourself fatigued and less efficient. To counteract this, **creative coach Mark McGuinness** suggests implementing a work routine that prioritizes your own creative work before responding to emails.

Furthermore, it is crucial to integrate regular breaks and ensure sufficient sleep to maximize your body's available energy. While the ideal amount of sleep varies for individuals, it is worth considering that only a small percentage (2.5%) of the population functions optimally with less than seven hours of sleep. Therefore, establishing a routine that allows for at least seven hours of quality sleep each night is highly beneficial, replacing reliance on excessive caffeine consumption.

Additionally, incorporating breaks into your work routine is essential. Research indicates that peak functioning can be sustained for approximately 90 minutes at a time. Taking periodic pauses and allowing yourself to relax enables you to recharge and maintain productivity levels.

While technology is designed to assist us, it is important not to let it dominate our lives. Smartphones and other devices, while convenient, can exert control over our behavior. However, it is crucial to recognize that we do not need to be constantly connected. **Author and**

**filmmaker James Victor** questions the necessity of carrying smartphones everywhere.

Consider whether excessive smartphone use is worth compromising good manners. In situations like a date, it is advisable to put your phone on airplane mode, allowing for uninterrupted personal interactions.

Technology can be tempting and hard to resist when it is readily available. It is akin to sitting next to a plate of delicious cookies while on a diet. To combat this, it is essential to turn off devices that may distract you when focusing on important tasks. If necessary, find a separate room or designated space to minimize technological temptations.

The expectation of constant availability, perpetuated by the convenience of technology, can be overwhelming. **Professor of Psychology Dan Ariely** even proposes implementing measures within companies to delay email delivery, preventing incessant bombardment. While widespread implementation of such processes may not be feasible, individually taking control by turning off devices or seeking uninterrupted spaces can significantly enhance focus.

**Enhance Your Creativity through Relaxation and New Hobbies**

Engaging in relaxation and adopting new hobbies can have a significant impact on boosting your creativity. By allowing yourself time for exercise and adequate rest, you will discover that your creative abilities are revitalized. As we have already learned, rest and sleep are vital components of a productive lifestyle. Moreover, they play a crucial role in generating creative ideas.

**Never stop asking questions**

Do you ever consider how many questions you ask each day? Perhaps you could benefit from asking a few more, as questions serve as the catalyst for an inquisitive and voracious mind. It is worth noting that every answer is preceded by a question.

The act of asking questions is fundamental to unraveling the information and insights you seek. Unfortunately, it is not a skill easily acquired through instruction alone; rather, it requires firsthand experience to appreciate the power of thought-provoking questions and develop proficiency in asking them.

Therefore, it is crucial to regard the art of question-asking as a valuable skill that can be honed through consistent practice. Make a conscious effort to prevent this skill from growing dull, and actively engage in the process of sharpening your ability to ask meaningful and impactful questions. By doing so, you unlock the gateway to a world of knowledge and understanding.

**Make an effort to gather knowledge – it will make you more creative and curious.**

Dedicating yourself to acquiring knowledge is a transformative endeavor that amplifies both your creativity and curiosity. In fact, it serves as an essential foundation upon which the edifice of creativity can be constructed.

As you have come to understand, creativity flourishes through the formation of innovative connections between seemingly unrelated thoughts and ideas. Consequently, the depth and breadth of your knowledge directly influence your capacity to forge these intricate connections.

Consider the illustrious playwright **William Shakespeare** as an exemplar. Scholars attest to his education at a classical school, where he delved into the realms of Greek and Latin and immersed himself in the works of luminaries such as Seneca and Cicero. This vast reservoir of knowledge served as the wellspring for his ability to craft plays spanning diverse themes, set in different times and locations. For instance, **Romeo and Juliet** unfolded in the distant city of Verona, Italy, far removed from Shakespeare's own abode in London.

Moreover, curiosity, akin to creativity, thrives on a bedrock of knowledge and facts. The more you acquaint yourself with a subject, the more acutely aware you become of the vast expanse of uncharted territories awaiting exploration. These gaps in information fuel your curiosity, propelling you on an unyielding quest for deeper understanding.

Therefore, make a concerted effort to embrace the pursuit of knowledge, recognizing its transformative power to propel your creative endeavors and nurture an insatiable curiosity that perpetually seeks to unravel the mysteries of the world.

## Create a "Life List" to Chart Your Path

A valuable approach to discerning your true aspirations in life is to envision your idealized, perfect day and subsequently compile a "life list" encompassing the experiences and achievements you aspire to accomplish. By linking the framework of your ideal day, such as dedicating a significant portion of your time to writing, with overarching objectives like publishing a remarkable novel within the next two years, you can establish a cohesive roadmap to guide your journey.

Take a moment to contemplate your perfect day, painting a vivid picture of the activities, accomplishments, and joys that would make it truly exceptional. Then, distill this vision into a tangible "life list" that encapsulates the aspirations you aim to fulfill at various stages of your existence. This exercise will align the structure of your ideal day with the broader scope of your goals, ensuring a harmonious synergy between the daily pursuit of your passions and the overarching milestones you strive to reach.

Whether it involves traveling to a particular destination, acquiring new skills, or realizing personal and professional ambitions, your "life list" serves as a compass, guiding you towards a life enriched by purposeful endeavors and fulfilling achievements.

## Create a "To-Stop-Doing List" to Reclaim Your Time

If you find yourself caught in a cycle of unproductive tasks and unnecessary distractions, consider crafting a "to-stop-doing list" as a powerful method to regain control of your time. Identify three to five activities that drain your energy without providing fulfillment or benefiting others and commit to eliminating them from your routine. You may be pleasantly surprised to discover that many of these tasks can be relinquished without significant consequences. By freeing yourself from these burdens, you will create valuable space for engaging in projects and activities that genuinely bring you joy.

Take a moment to reflect on your current commitments and obligations, focusing on tasks that weigh you down or offer little value in return. These might include unproductive habits, time-consuming obligations, or unnecessary distractions. Compile these items on your "to-stop-doing list" as a tangible reminder of the activities you have chosen to let go of. By consciously releasing these draining tasks, you will liberate precious time and energy to invest in pursuits that align with your passions and bring you genuine satisfaction.

**Don't force your art to pay your rent.**

Instead of compromising your artistic integrity, consider supporting your creative career by maintaining a day job. It may seem like a compromise or a lack of full commitment to your art, but finding a balance between your job and your artistic pursuits can fuel greater passion. Think of it as having a secret affair with your art!

Take inspiration from acclaimed authors like **Toni Morrison and J.K. Rowling**, who initially nurtured their writing as clandestine affairs. By carving out stolen moments from their regular lives, they granted themselves the time and space needed to write. These dedicated hours can become cherished rituals, sustaining our creative drive even when the daily grind becomes overwhelming.

By keeping your day job, you also create a safety net that allows for creative freedom. Artistic success is never guaranteed, so why burden your art with the expectation of financial gain or fame? Excessive pressure can drain the joy from your creative process. To create with unrestrained passion and without fear of disappointing yourself, provide yourself with the security to explore your artistry, knowing you have other options to rely on.

## Start today!

No matter what your aspirations are, dedicate yourself fully to them every single day. Failing to do so will only lead to regret in the long run. A friend of the author once remarked that cemeteries hold the most valuable land on Earth, as they are filled with immeasurable amounts of untapped potential and unrealized ideas. By implementing the strategies outlined in these insights and consistently striving to unleash your full potential, you can ensure that you "die empty." So, dare to start your creative journey today!

★ ★ ★ ★ ★

# Chapter 9: Top 51 Creative Inspirational Ideas

**********

**"The future belongs to those who believe in the beauty of their dreams."**

**~ Eleanor Roosevelt**

1. Eliminate unnecessary things in your life to make room for what you really want to do.

2. Focus on creating legacy work that will make the world a better place.

3. Create a "life list" to keep you focused on your goals.

4. Make a "to-stop-doing list" to remove distractions.

5. Find your flow and allow yourself to fully immerse in your creative work.

6. Tap into the inspiring magic of creativity to unleash your potential.

7. Learn to recognize when an idea is calling out to you.

8.  Don't rely on your art to pay the bills; create for the sake of creating.

9.  Focus is key to unlocking creative insights.

10. Forge strong relationships to combat the loneliness of creative work.

11. Seek out diverse and challenging stimuli to keep your creativity flowing.

12. The quality, not quantity, of your creative work is what matters.

13. Don't buy into the myth that creativity is reserved for a select few.

14. Collaborate, revise, and combine ideas to create something truly unique.

15. Writing regularly and trying new things can help you connect with your creative side.

16. Ideas already exist in the universe; it's your job to nurture and develop them.

17. Avoid perfectionism, work alcoholism, and competitiveness, which can stifle creativity.

18. Make a conscious effort to express your creative self.

19. Prioritize and make time for your creative pursuits and create an environment that supports them.

20. Embrace your inner artist and let it guide your creativity.

21. Open yourself up to creative inspiration from various sources.

22. Pay attention to what you are consuming and how it affects your creativity.

23. Push past fear and take action to realize your creative vision.

24. Bring your ideas to life by turning them into reality.

25. Celebrate your deep creativity and the unique perspective it brings.

26. Nature can be a source of inspiration and help to recharge your creativity.

27. Nurture a relationship with your creative impulse to keep it alive.

28. Embrace and honor your creative impulse, no matter where it takes you.

29. Big ideas are often made up of smaller thoughts that build up over time.

30. Continuously generate new ideas and give them time to grow and develop.

31. The myth of the child prodigy is just that - a myth.

32. Age does not diminish creativity; in fact, it can often be a source of renewed energy.

33. Take time to observe the world around you and find inspiration in the everyday.

34. Personalize your workspace to enhance your creativity and productivity.

35. Overcome fear and negative mindsets by taking small, concrete steps towards your goals.

36. Let your inner child lead the way in your creative process.

37. Stay motivated by visualizing your ideal future and learning from past mistakes.

38. Disconnect from technology regularly to give your mind a break.

39. Learn from your creative heroes by imitating and emulating their work.

40. Share your work with others but enjoy the benefits of obscurity first.

41. Create an inspiring workspace for yourself, but also make time to get out and experience the world.

42. Value praise and constructive feedback, but don't let criticism bring you down.

43. Each of us has a Personal Legend waiting to be fulfilled.

44. Build a daily routine that aligns with your body's natural rhythms and creative pursuits.

45. Use technology to your advantage, but don't let it control your life.

46. Taking time to relax and pursue hobbies can help boost your creativity.

47. Your mind can be your greatest obstacle to achieving your creative goals.

48. Take your questions for a walk to stimulate your
mind and find inspiration.

49. We all have the capacity for creativity – we just
need to practice it.

50. Never stop asking questions.

51. Anything can be interesting with the right
perspective.

# Chapter 10: Full Book Summary

**************

**"The best way to predict the future is to invent it."**

**~ Alan Kay**

## Chapter 1- Introduction: Key Takeaways

The chapter opens with a creative thinking story from centuries ago, showcasing the clever problem-solving abilities of a woman named Jennifer. Faced with a manipulative moneylender who presented her with a rigged choice, Jennifer's out-of-the-box thinking, and quick wit led to a favorable outcome that freed her father from debt and avoided an unwanted marriage.

The chapter then moves on to real-life examples of renowned creative geniuses, starting with Steve Jobs. Jobs' story highlights his innovative mindset, determination, and willingness to take risks. The chapter emphasizes his transformative contributions to the technology industry, particularly through inventions like the iPod and iPhone. Jobs' legacy serves as a reminder that passion, perseverance, and a commitment to excellence are crucial for creative success.

The next featured creative genius is Elon Musk, whose unconventional thinking and relentless pursuit of his passions have revolutionized various industries. From his early days as a self-taught coder to his ventures in companies like SpaceX, Tesla, and Solar City, Musk's journey demonstrates the power of imagination and determination in driving innovation.

The chapter concludes by discussing the book's purpose and what readers can expect to gain from it. Rather than solely focusing on creative thinking stories, the author recognizes readers' desire to develop their own creative thinking skills. The book promises to demystify the concept of creativity, provide practical exercises and tips to enhance creative thinking abilities, and offer guidance on applying creativity to problem-solving and innovation. It emphasizes the potential for personal and professional growth through the development of a creative mindset.

The chapter ends by encouraging readers to adopt a broader perspective on creativity and its possibilities. It assures them that the strategies presented in the book are not novel but have been utilized by creative thinkers throughout history. Creative thinking is portrayed as a valuable skill accessible to everyone, capable of generating remarkable results in various fields.

## Chapter 2- The Nature of Creativity: Key Takeaways

The chapter begins with an inspiring story of Leonardo da Vinci, highlighting his curiosity, passion, and determination in pursuing art, science, and invention. Despite facing challenges and setbacks, da Vinci's ability to connect science with art made him one of the greatest creative geniuses in history.

The chapter then delves into the understanding of creativity. It explains that creativity involves coming up with ideas that are both novel and useful, and it extends beyond artistic expression to encompass fields such as science, business, and social issues. Creativity can be developed and nurtured through methods like lateral thinking, mind mapping, and brainstorming, and it plays a significant role in innovation and advancement in various domains.

The creative process is explored in detail, breaking it down into several key steps. These steps include preparation, incubation, inspiration, evaluation, implementation, and reflection. Each step is explained, emphasizing the importance of acquiring knowledge, allowing ideas to incubate, experiencing moments of inspiration, evaluating, and refining ideas, implementing them in tangible forms, and reflecting on the creative process for future growth.

The chapter also addresses the question of whether creativity is a natural talent or a skill that can be learned. It is highlighted that while some individuals may have a greater natural inclination towards creativity, it is a skill that can be acquired and honed through practice and exposure to diverse experiences and concepts.

Different types of creativity are discussed, including creative imagination, creativity in science and technology, entrepreneurship, social innovation, and personal creativity. It is emphasized that individuals can express their creativity in various fields throughout their lives, and these categories are not mutually exclusive.

The chapter further explores the factors that influence creative success, such as knowledge and ability, resilience and perseverance, motivation and enthusiasm, flexibility and adaptability, a supportive and collaborative environment, experimentation and risk-taking, and uniqueness and originality.

Several business case studies are provided to illustrate the importance of creativity in the success of organizations. The stories of Apple, McDonald's, 3M, and Kodak highlight how creativity and the ability to embrace new ideas and adapt to change can determine the fate of a business.

The chapter concludes by dispelling the misconception that creativity is limited to a select few. It emphasizes that everyone possesses creative potential and suggests practical steps to nurture creativity, including engaging in morning pages, going on artist dates, and exploring the world with curiosity and openness.

## Chapter 3- Overcoming Creative Blocks: Key Takeaways

This chapter explores various methods to overcome creative blocks and resume productivity and creativity. The chapter begins by emphasizing the importance of understanding what a creative block is and why it occurs. It highlights that stress, burnout, failure fear, and lack of inspiration can contribute to creative blocks. By identifying the root causes of a creative block, individuals can develop strategies to overcome them.

The chapter suggests that taking a break from the project can be an effective way to overcome a creative block. Stepping away and engaging in activities like going for a walk, listening to music, or reading a book can help refresh the mind and refuel creativity. It also discusses the benefits of vacations and downtime in generating new ideas and fostering creativity.

Changing one's surroundings is another strategy to overcome a creative block. By altering the environment or workspace, individuals can stimulate their brain and spark new ideas. The chapter also encourages adopting a childlike approach to creativity, embracing curiosity, and asking questions to gain a deeper understanding of challenges. Imagining alternative perspectives and incorporating fun and enjoyment in the workplace are also highlighted as ways to strengthen creativity.

Finding inspiration from various sources such as art, nature, music, and conversations with others is presented as a powerful tool to overcome creative blocks. The chapter emphasizes the importance of emotions in decision-making and the role of confidence, planning, and consistent practice in nurturing creativity. Collaborating with others and incorporating solo brainstorming sessions are discussed as ways to fuel creativity and generate innovative ideas.

Practicing mindfulness is presented as a technique to reduce stress and anxiety, which are common causes of creative blocks. Mindfulness exercises like meditation, yoga, and deep breathing can help individuals achieve clarity and focus, leading to improved creativity. Setting modest goals, trying out new methods and brainstorming techniques, and breaking free from routine thinking are additional strategies explored in the chapter.

This chapter provides practical advice and insights into overcoming creative blocks and fostering a creative mindset. By understanding the causes of creative blocks and employing these strategies, you can unlock their creative potential and continue their creative journey.

## Chapter 4- Cultivating a Creative Mindset: Key Takeaways

In this chapter, the importance of developing a creative mindset and the practices of highly creative individuals are explored.

The chapter begins with the inspiring story of J.K. Rowling, the author of the Harry Potter series, who faced numerous challenges and setbacks but persisted in pursuing her passion for writing. Rowling's life and work serve as an example of perseverance, creativity, and using one's talents to make a positive impact on the world.

The chapter then delves into various strategies and habits that can help cultivate a creative mindset. It emphasizes the importance of curiosity and embracing new experiences to fuel creativity. It encourages the practice of divergent thinking, which involves generating multiple solutions and exploring unconventional ideas. Developing a daily routine and rituals that stimulate creativity is also recommended.

The chapter highlights the role of failure in the creative process and encourages embracing failure as an opportunity for growth and learning. It suggests taking risks, stepping outside of one's comfort zone, and reframing failures as learning experiences.

Creating a positive environment that supports and uplifts creativity is another important aspect discussed in the chapter. Surrounding oneself with supportive individuals and engaging in self-reflection exercises can help enhance creativity.

The chapter concludes with the idea of directing focus towards creating work that leaves a lasting impact and contributes to a better world. It encourages readers to break free from conformity, embrace uncertainty, and allow their minds to wander and daydream to generate new ideas.

It provides valuable insights and practical tips for cultivating a creative mindset, encouraging readers to tap into their creative potential and make a positive difference through their work.

## Chapter 5- Secrets to Creative Genius: Key Takeaways

While there is no one-size-fits-all approach to becoming a creative genius, there are common characteristics that many creative geniuses possess.

The chapter begins by highlighting Oprah Winfrey as a prime example of a creative and innovative individual. Oprah's success stems from her willingness to take risks and explore new avenues. Starting as a news anchor, she discovered her passion for connecting with people and telling their stories, leading her to create her own talk show, The Oprah Winfrey Show. Oprah's creativity extended beyond her talk show, as she launched her own production company, Harpo Productions, and cable network, OWN, giving voice to diverse perspectives.

Oprah's ability to empathize and tell stories sets her apart as a creative inspiration. She tackles challenging subjects and changes the conversation on important issues like race, gender, and sexual orientation. Additionally, her commitment to personal growth and self-improvement has been instrumental in overcoming obstacles and advocating for mental and emotional well-being.

The chapter emphasizes that each creative genius possesses their unique set of qualities, and there is no standard formula for becoming one. However, it outlines several characteristics that highly creative people often share:

**Open-mindedness**: Creative geniuses are receptive to new experiences, ideas, and feedback. They question their own beliefs and assumptions.

**Imagination**: These individuals possess vivid imaginations, enabling them to see things from unique perspectives and imagine possibilities others might overlook. They maintain a lifelong curiosity, constantly seeking new experiences and asking questions.

**Persistence**: Creativity often involves trial and error. Creative geniuses exhibit perseverance and invest the time and effort required to develop their ideas. They are undeterred by failure or setbacks.

**Willingness to experiment**: Taking risks and trying new things is essential for creativity. Creative geniuses embrace uncertainty, are comfortable with ambiguity, and are unafraid to solve problems in unconventional ways.

**Passion**: Creative geniuses are deeply committed to their work, driven by a genuine love for what they do. They have a strong sense of purpose and are motivated internally rather than by external rewards.

**Solid work ethic**: Creativity requires hard work and dedication. Creative geniuses strike a balance between their creative impulses and the discipline necessary to bring their ideas to fruition.

**Playfulness**: Many creative geniuses approach their work with a playful and fun attitude. They enjoy experimentation, making mistakes, and maintaining a childlike sense of wonder.

**Spirit of collaboration**: Creative geniuses thrive in collaborative settings and excel at recognizing connections between seemingly unrelated concepts. They integrate ideas from different fields in innovative ways.

**Thinking across disciplines**: Highly creative individuals often possess diverse interests, abilities, and experiences, which they draw upon in their work.

In conclusion, creativity is a multifaceted and unique phenomenon, making it impossible to provide a definitive formula for achieving creative genius. However, cultivating certain characteristics and habits, as exemplified by Oprah Winfrey, can help individuals tap into their creative potential. Open-mindedness, imagination, persistence, willingness to experiment, passion, a solid work ethic, playfulness, a spirit of collaboration, and thinking across disciplines are all qualities that can contribute to unleashing one's own unique form of creative genius.

# Chapter 6- Innovating in the Digital Age: Key Takeaways

In today's digital age, innovation plays a crucial role in achieving success. This chapter explores the impact of technology on the creative process and how it can be harnessed to drive success and accomplish creative goals.

The digital landscape is ever-changing, with new technologies emerging rapidly. Staying up to date with the latest trends and recognizing the opportunities they offer is essential for understanding this landscape. Social media platforms, online collaboration tools, digital design software, and artificial intelligence (AI) applications are among the tools and resources available in the digital landscape.

Social media has become an integral part of the creative process, providing platforms for idea sharing, networking, and audience building. Creatives can connect with their communities, promote their work, and gather feedback. Social media also serves as a research and inspiration tool, enabling creatives to explore new concepts and stay updated on industry trends.

Online collaboration has gained popularity due to remote work and digital collaboration tools. Real-time collaboration regardless of location allows for idea sharing, brainstorming, and project collaboration. Project management software, online whiteboards, and video conferencing tools facilitate online collaboration.

Artificial intelligence (AI) has revolutionized the creative process, offering opportunities for automation, analysis, and innovation. AI applications can generate groundbreaking ideas, automate tasks, and provide insights. AI's impact is seen in various AI-powered apps like **Chat GPT, Bard, Bing, and virtual assistants**. Chat GPT enables interactive conversations with a language model, Bard assists in music composition, Bing offers intelligent search results, and virtual assistants like **Siri and Alexa** streamline daily tasks.

Agile methodologies, emphasizing adaptability, teamwork, and rapid iteration, are gaining traction in the creative process. Agile project management breaks tasks into manageable parts and uses short sprints for goal achievement and feedback gathering, fostering creativity and flexibility.

Experimentation with new technologies is an essential part of innovation in the digital age. Being open to new tools and platforms and exploring novel ways of working and collaborating can lead to new insights and opportunities.

However, digital innovation also comes with challenges. It is crucial to be aware of risks and take precautions to safeguard intellectual property and data privacy. Avoiding digital burnout and maintaining a healthy balance are also important considerations.

In the digital age, embracing technology, utilizing social media, online collaboration, AI, agile methodologies, experimenting with new technologies, and navigating digital challenges are key to driving creative success and achieving objectives.

The digital age offers a wealth of opportunities for innovation, and by harnessing the power of technology, individuals and teams can unleash their creative potential and thrive in this new era of creativity.

## Chapter 7- Habits of Highly Creative People: Key Takeaways

The chapter begins with the story of Michael Phelps, an Olympic swimmer known for his determination and mental toughness. Phelps overcame challenges and used his creativity and innovation not only in swimming but also in raising awareness about mental health and promoting environmental causes.

The chapter challenges the common belief that creativity is elusive and reserved for a select few. It debunks the myth of left-brain versus right-brain dominance in creativity, explaining that the creative process involves the whole brain, with different regions working together. It emphasizes that everyone is born creative but often loses it as they grow up.

The chapter then highlights several habits commonly associated with creative individuals. First, embracing curiosity and constantly seeking new experiences, ideas, and perspectives. Creative people are keen observers of the world around them and pay attention to details that others might overlook. They have an insatiable hunger for knowledge, which provides them with fresh ideas.

Second, creative people nurture their passion and use it as fuel to stay motivated. They prioritize activities aligned with their values and interests, striking a balance between inspiration and hard work.

Third, creative individuals are comfortable with ambiguity and take risks. They embrace uncertainty and view it as an opportunity to explore and discover new ideas. They are not afraid to question assumptions and challenge the status quo.

Fourth, creative people are committed to developing their skills and knowledge in their chosen field. They prioritize their creative work, practice regularly, and make time for creative thinking.

Fifth, collaboration is crucial for creativity. Highly creative individuals often work with others to generate new ideas and perspectives. Collaboration and diverse perspectives can lead to innovative breakthroughs.

Sixth, creative people stay flexible and adaptable. They are open to new ideas and willing to change course if necessary. They embrace uncertainty and failure as steppingstones to innovation.

Seventh, engaging in play is an important part of the creative process. Cultivating a childlike sense of play allows individuals to experiment, explore, and trigger new solutions.

Eighth, having a process is essential for creativity. Creativity is not just a big flash of insight but a deliberate process that anyone can follow.

Ninth, taking hobbies seriously can have a positive impact on creativity. Hobbies provide complementary mental and emotional experiences that help individuals perform better in their core jobs.

Finally, generating a lot of ideas is important for creativity. Creative people have divergent thinking patterns, allowing them to generate multiple possibilities and combine different ideas to create unexpected combinations.

The chapter concludes by mentioning the benefits of practicing mindfulness, as it helps individuals become more present and focused, enhancing their ability to generate creative ideas.

Overall, the chapter highlights that creativity is not reserved for a select few but can be cultivated through habits and behaviors that foster a mindset of curiosity, passion, flexibility, collaboration, and play. By adopting these habits, individuals can unleash their creative genius and overcome obstacles to achieve greatness in their chosen fields.

## Chapter 8- Living a Creative Life Everyday: Key Takeaways

It tells the story of a remarkable individual named Amelia, who had a passion for creativity and believed that it was not just a hobby but a way of life.

Amelia's creative spirit was initially dimmed by the pressures of society, but she refused to let the world define her worth or suppress her creative genius. She made a pact with herself to live a creative life every day, no matter what.

Amelia embarked on a journey of self-discovery and creative awakening. She sought out like-minded individuals, joined art communities, and immersed herself in the creative energy that surrounded her. Amelia understood that creativity was not just about creating; it was a mindset that involved seeing inspiration in the mundane and finding beauty in the ordinary.

She embraced failure as a steppingstone to success and celebrated her mistakes as valuable lessons. Amelia realized that the journey of a creative person was not always smooth, but it was the bumps and detours that made it rewarding.

As Amelia continued her creative path, she not only created for herself but also for others. She discovered the profound impact her work could have on the world, touching hearts, provoking thoughts, and inspiring change. Amelia's commitment to living a creative life every day became contagious as she encouraged others to embrace their own creative spark.

The chapter also discusses practical tips for bringing creativity to life, such as setting objectives and a clear vision, choosing the necessary resources, fostering a plan, developing a creative mindset, organizing a team, and effective communication. It emphasizes the importance of acting, assessing performance, and making adjustments along the way.

Furthermore, the chapter explores the concept of embracing the flow of creative inspiration by cultivating awareness and a connection with nature. It highlights the significance of nurturing a relationship with the creative impulse and celebrating one's unique perspective. The chapter also emphasizes the importance of creating an inspiring work environment, balancing space, and exploration, disconnecting from technology, and nurturing hobbies and side projects alongside the artistic journey.

## Chapter 9- Top 51 Creative Inspirational Ideas: Key Takeaways

The chapter presents **51 creative inspirational ideas** to help readers unlock their creative potential and bring their unique visions to life.

The chapter begins by emphasizing the importance of eliminating unnecessary elements from one's life to create space for meaningful creative pursuits. It encourages readers to focus on creating work that will leave a legacy and contribute to making the world a better place.

To stay on track with their goals, readers are advised to create a "life list" and a "to-stop-doing list." These tools help maintain focus and remove distractions that may hinder creative progress. The chapter also emphasizes the significance of finding one's flow, immersing oneself in creative work, and tapping into the inspiring magic of creativity.

Recognizing when an idea is calling out and heeding that call is discussed as a crucial aspect of the creative process. The chapter advises against relying on art solely to pay the bills, highlighting the importance of creating for the sake of creation itself.

Maintaining focus is identified as a key factor in unlocking creative insights, while fostering strong relationships can combat the potential loneliness associated with creative work. Seeking out diverse and challenging stimuli is encouraged to keep creativity flowing, emphasizing the quality rather than the quantity of creative output.

The chapter dispels the myth that creativity is reserved for a select few, emphasizing that collaboration, revision, and combination of ideas can lead to truly unique creations. Regular writing and trying new things are suggested to connect with one's creative side.

Readers are reminded that ideas already exist in the universe, and it is their role to nurture and develop them. Perfectionism, workaholic, competitiveness, and other hindrances to creativity are to be avoided. The chapter advises making a conscious effort to express one's creative self and creating an environment that supports creative pursuits.

Drawing inspiration from various sources, being mindful of the impact of consumption on creativity, and acting despite fear are encouraged. The chapter emphasizes the importance of bringing ideas to life and celebrating the deep creativity and unique perspective everyone possesses.

Nature is highlighted as a source of inspiration and rejuvenation, while nurturing the relationship with one's creative impulse is seen as essential. The chapter suggests that big ideas are often built upon smaller thoughts that develop over time.

Age is acknowledged as not diminishing creativity but rather providing renewed energy. The chapter encourages readers to observe the world around them and find inspiration in everyday life. Personalizing workspaces, overcoming fear and negative mindsets, and embracing the influence of the inner child are discussed as means to enhance creativity.

Staying motivated through visualization, learning from past mistakes, and periodically disconnecting from technology are suggested practices. The chapter advises learning from creative heroes, sharing work with others, and valuing constructive feedback. It reinforces the belief that everyone possesses a Personal Legend waiting to be fulfilled.

Aligning daily routines with natural rhythms and creative pursuits is recommended, and while technology can be advantageous, it should not control one's life. Relaxation and pursuing hobbies are recognized as beneficial for boosting creativity. Overcoming mental obstacles, taking questions for a walk to find inspiration, and the importance of continuous practice are also explored.

The chapter concludes by urging readers to never stop asking questions and highlights the potential interest that can be found in any subject with the right perspective. By embracing these strategies and perspectives, readers can unleash their creative potential and embark on a fulfilling creative journey.

# Conclusion



**"Creativity takes courage."**

**~Henri Matisse**

Congratulations on reaching the conclusion of "Unleash Your Inner Creative Genius." It is truly an accomplishment to have journeyed through this book and explored the depths of creativity and innovation. I commend you for your commitment and dedication to self-improvement.

Throughout the pages of this book, we have unraveled the various facets of creativity, challenging common misconceptions and revealing its true essence. We have discovered that creativity is not a selfish pursuit but a fundamental aspect of living a truly fulfilling life.

By exploring different techniques, exercises, and perspectives, you have gained the tools necessary to nurture and harness your creative abilities. Remember that creativity knows no boundaries and can be applied to every aspect of your life, whether personal or professional.

Embracing your inner creative genius is not a one-time achievement but an ongoing journey. It requires consistent practice, an open mind, and a willingness to take risks. As you venture forth, I encourage you to stay curious, embrace failure as a stepping stone to success, and surround yourself with like-minded individuals who support and inspire your creative endeavors.

Your newfound understanding of creativity can extend beyond your own life. Share your knowledge and experiences with others, encouraging them to tap into their own creative potential. By doing so, you become a catalyst for positive change and inspiration in the lives of those around you.

Always remember that creativity is a deeply personal and unique expression of yourself. Trust your instincts, follow your passions, and allow your creativity to guide you towards a more vibrant and fulfilling existence.

As you continue your journey of self-discovery and creative exploration, may you find endless joy, inspiration, and fulfillment in embracing your inner creative genius. Your creativity has the power to shape not only your life but also the world around you.

Thank you once again for joining me on this transformative journey. I wish you the very best in your endeavors to unleash your inner creative genius and create a life filled with innovation, beauty, and boundless possibilities.

With warmest regards,

Girendra Nath Singh
Author of "Unleash Your Inner Creative Genius"

# DISCLAIMER

This book is intended for entertainment purposes only. Readers are advised that the author does not provide legal, financial, medical, or professional advice. The content in this book has been curated from diverse sources. Prior to attempting any techniques outlined, readers are encouraged to consult licensed professionals.

By engaging with this material, readers agree that the author is not liable for any direct or indirect losses resulting from the use of the information contained herein, including errors, omissions, or inaccuracies. Compliance with all pertinent laws and regulations, spanning international, federal, state, and local jurisdictions, is the sole responsibility of the reader. Neither the author nor the publisher assumes any responsibility or liability for the reader's use of these materials. Any unintended offense to individuals or organizations is regrettable and unintentional.

*******

# ABOUT THE AUTHOR

 Meet the visionary mind behind **"The Happiness Amplifier,"** *Mr. Girendra Nath Singh* is a distinguished Electrical Engineer with an MBA. Mr. Singh brings over three decades of hands-on industrial experience, both in India and abroad, to the forefront of his remarkable literary journey.

With a genuine desire to make a lasting impact, Mr. Singh's unique blend of technical expertise and unwavering dedication is woven into every page of his book. His commitment to crafting insightful narratives that resonate with readers is evident in **"The Happiness Amplifier,"** where he seamlessly bridges the realms of **psychology, neuroscience, and real-life experiences.**

**Other books Mr. Singh has written:**
**The Happiness Amplifier**

https://books2read.com/u/4EpoKe

# Your Free Gift

As a token of my thanks for taking time to read my book, I would like to offer you a free gift:

Click Here or scan the below QR Code & Receive your Free Book:

https://gnsingh.ck.page/79606d929c

# Thank You and a Small Request

Dear Reader,

I want to extend my heartfelt gratitude to you for journeying through the pages of **"Unleash Your Inner Creative genius".** Your decision to explore this book warms my heart, and I sincerely hope it has enriched your understanding of happiness and its intricate tapestry.

***May I kindly request a brief moment of your time?***
Taking a moment to leave a review is a simple yet impactful act that can shape the future of this book and the lives it touches. Please consider sharing your reflections on the platform where you obtained your copy.

Your support is a beacon of encouragement, and I am genuinely excited to read your thoughts and experiences. Thank you for being a part of this voyage towards lasting joy.

With heartfelt appreciation,

**Girendra Nath Singh
Author**

**"This is not the end, this is not even the beginning of the end, and this is just perhaps the end of the beginning." ~ Winston S. Churchill**

**********